THE
HUMAN
SEXES

THE HUMAN SEXES

A Natural History of Man and Woman

DESMOND MORRIS

ST. MARTIN'S PRESS   NEW YORK

For Silke

This book is published to accompany the
television series entitled *The Human Sexes*
which was produced by Partridge Films for
The Learning Channel. The series producer
was Clive Bromhall.

ISBN 0 312 18311 9
First published in Great Britain by BBC Worldwide Ltd.

First Edition
10 9 8 7 6 5 4 3 2 1

Contents

Introduction *page 6*

1 Male and Female *page 10*

2 Language of the Sexes *page 40*

3 Patterns of Love *page 82*

4 Passages of Life *page 126*

5 The Maternal Dilemma *page 168*

6 The Gender Wars *page 194*

Afterword *page 242*

Bibliography *page 244*

Acknowledgements *page 249*

Picture Credits *page 250*

Index *page 251*

Introduction

There can be little doubt that, for over a million years, our ancient ancestors existed in a state of sexual equality. This does not mean that males and females were the same. Far from it: there was an increasing division of labour between the sexes and this division led to deep-seated, inborn differences. There may have been a gender balance, but there was no gender blurring.

In a hundred small ways – some in anatomy, some in behaviour – males became more male and females became more female. It is important to explore these differences in order to understand the perfect balance they can offer in an ideal human environment. It is also important to investigate the ways in which this balance has been disturbed by modern life.

Before farming replaced hunting as the basic survival system of our species, the balance of the sexes was safe enough. The men went off to hunt and the women remained close to the tribal settlement. The men killed prey animals and returned home with the spoils. The women gathered vegetable food. Their separate efforts combined neatly to provide the richly varied diet on which our ancestors not only survived, but thrived, multiplied and spread out to cover most of the globe.

Then, about 10,000 years ago, the vegetable gathering was made more efficient by planting crops. This concentrated the food supply, but it also attracted many large herbivores such as wild cattle, sheep and goats, which became serious pests, devouring the crops and robbing the farmers of their new-found advantage.

The answer was simple – the animals attracted to the crops were trapped, penned in, killed and eaten. Now there was no need to set off on the chase. The prey was coming in of its own accord. Even better, once trapped, these prey animals could be kept alive until another meal was required. The old 'feast and famine' pendulum swings of primeval hunting life became a fading memory.

It is important to try and get inside the head of the opposite sex, when studying gender relationships. ('The Face of Mae West That Can Be Used As a Drawing Room' by Salvador Dali.)

Soon, a vital new step was taken. Some of the trapped animals were pregnant and gave birth. It dawned on the early farmers that this could be exploited. What if they kept some of them alive and bred from them in captivity, only killing off the surplus? Domesticated livestock and animal husbandry had arrived.

Now there was a food surplus and food security of a kind undreamed of by the primeval hunters of earlier times. Before long, food stores made it possible for small settlements to grow into large villages, villages to swell into market towns, and towns to spread into huge cities. In a mere 10,000 years, the bright lights of modern civilization had emerged out of the darkness of primitive tribal existence. There had been no time for human beings to evolve into a new species of urban animal. The city-dwellers, in their smart suits, fast cars and insulated dwellings, were biologically identical to the Stone Age people who painted hunting scenes on the walls of caves. They possessed the same anatomy and were driven by the same urges. Only their lifestyles had changed. And what a dramatic change it was.

In the past, women had been at the heart of social life, while the men were largely out on the periphery in the hunting grounds. Now the tables had been turned. Urban life unfairly favoured the males. Their new, symbolic hunting took place in the city centre while the females were confined to breeding dormitories in the suburbs. They were no longer at the heart of society, but on its fringes. Eventually, in modern times, they rebelled against this unnatural bias, attempting to regain their ancient, natural sexual equality in a new way. If urban life favoured the males and made them the dominant sex in society, then the females would join them. If the male work ethic was so rewarding, they would have it too. Their brains were as good as those of the males, so all that was necessary was to overcome the masculine prejudices that suffused modern culture.

In some parts of the world the females succeeded, but not without cost. In other parts they failed and remain unfairly exploited and suppressed to this day. Even in those regions where they did succeed, their campaigns led them to an uncomfortable victory. Instead of regaining their original, natural form of equality based on a balanced division of labour, they struggled towards a pseudo-male position, attempting to compete with males rather than succeed on their own, female terms.

This, in a nutshell, is the story of *The Human Sexes.* The first chapter explores the biological differences between the sexes and asks: just how different are men and women in their anatomy, their physiology, their senses and their brains? The second chapter takes a close look at the many ways in which different human cultures have varied these biological differences, exaggerating some features and suppressing others, to create the rich variety of human gender signals that we see today. The third chapter examines the different human mateship systems that exist and asks questions about the primary monogamy of our species and its relation to polygamy, promiscuity, prostitution, celibacy, homosexuality and solitary sex. The fourth chapter deals with the gender aspects of the typical human rites of passage, from birth to death. The fifth chapter takes a hard look at the maternal dilemma – how the modern human female can manage to find mental fulfilment while at the same time obeying her powerful maternal urges; a balance that was simple enough to achieve in primeval times, but is increasingly difficult in today's urban environment. In the final chapter, the controversial subject of the gender wars is confronted. What is happening to the relationship between the sexes today? And will the primeval harmony between the sexes ever be fully regained?

Throughout the book, every attempt is made to remain objective. This is not easy because, since I am male, there could easily be a tendency for me to favour the female in order to avoid accusations of masculine bias. Currying favour in this way – a fault of several recent male authors – is almost as offensive and irritating as the old-style 'male supremacy' approach. The plain fact is that human females are superior to males in some respects and inferior in others. Taken together, this gives a primeval sexual equality based on mutual aid, with the male specialities combining with the female specialities to create an efficient survival team. Any attempts to ignore this arrangement and to suggest that the sexes are identical in most respects, or that one sex is in general better than the other, have to be scrupulously avoided if the scientific truth about our species is to be told. I am aware that some of my remarks will offend one extremist campaigning group or another, but that is something I can live with if, in the process, I can illuminate the true nature of the human sexes.

1

Male and Female

All higher forms of life have one thing in common: their teeming populations are split in two, one half male, the other half female. But just how similar and how different is the opposite sex?

We are so familiar with the idea of contrasting males and females that we tend to take this arrangement for granted, but with some lower forms of life every individual is both male and female. When two of them mate, they inseminate one another and both become pregnant. However, with higher forms of life it is usually quite clear which individual is masculine and which is feminine. Not only do they have different reproductive systems, they also differ in a number of other ways. There is division of labour between the sexes, the male becoming specialized in one direction, the female in another. And this is just as true of the human animal as it is of other species.

To understand how human masculinity and femininity evolved, it would help if we could turn the clock back to observe our prehistoric ancestors. Sadly, we cannot do that. The best we can do is to take a look at a group of modern people who are still living the same sort of tribal, tropical existence today. This is not easy, because most such societies have been contaminated by modern cultures. Feather headdresses are accompanied by T-shirts; the bone worn in the nose is proudly replaced with a biro. But there are still a few tribes where the primeval way of life has somehow managed to survive such intrusions, which can give us some valuable clues about the relation between the sexes as it probably existed in ancient times.

In some regions, the pygmies of West Africa are still living as hunter-gatherers, even today. They survive much as their ancestors did, hundreds of thousands of years ago when our species was young. The role of the males is to hunt, to dismember the carcasses of the animals they kill

To appreciate the true nature of human gender differences, we have to understand the division of labour that developed during our evolution, with the females food-gathering (below) and the males hunting (above), as still happens today in some tribal cultures such as these West African pygmies.

and to design and construct their hunting weapons. The role of the females is to gather fruit, nuts, berries and fungi and to build the simple round huts whenever they move to a new camp site. Although the bulk of the food eaten comes from the women's activities, the meat provided by the men is of a much higher nutritional value. Allowing for this difference, it is true to say that the contribution of males and females to tribal nutrition is roughly equal. This equality of importance in feeding is reflected in an equality of importance in tribal matters generally. Decisions on male concerns are made by the men; decisions on female concerns are made by the women.

It is almost certain that, throughout our long evolutionary past, the human animal has thrived on this natural balance of power between the sexes, rather than on the domination of one sex by the other. 'Equal but different' could have been our human slogan. The question is, how different – and how is this reflected in our lives today?

Male Muscle

As men and women increasingly specialized in their respective tasks as hunters and gatherers, the most obvious difference was in muscular strength. To succeed at the hunt, the human male had to become bigger, stronger and more athletic. This primeval gender difference can be measured in a number of ways.

It begins at birth. The male baby is, on average, heavier and longer than the female baby. It also exhibits a higher basal metabolism – something it will have throughout its life – a feature that is suited to a more strenuous, active lifestyle. Newborn males show more vigorous limb movements, as if impatient to get started with their athletic pursuits. Also, their visual acuity is greater, heralding the time when, as adult hunters, they must survey the landscape for telltale signs of prey. Another difference is their interest in manipulating objects: male infants are more prone to bang and hammer toys, whereas females are more subdued in their play. Young boys are more interested in running, jumping, pushing and pulling; little girls tend to sit down and play with the objects in front of them. Infant boys are also more interested in investigating any new toy that is offered.

These differences all occur long before there can have been any adult influences or 'gender role' bias. They are clearly inborn and set the tiny boys and girls off on slightly different paths, which they will follow all their lives. The power-playing of the male infants is a clear precursor of their later muscular exploits. And their greater interest in novel objects – which might just be dangerous – is destined to mature into the greater adult risk-taking of the adult human male. All these features support the idea of a deep division of labour between the sexes in our species.

At adulthood, the body of the human male is, on average, 30 per cent stronger than that of the human female, with nearly twice the weight of muscular tissue. (The average male has 26 kg – over 57 lb – of muscle compared with 15 kg or 33 lb for the female.) A typical female can only carry half her weight, whereas a typical male can carry twice his weight. Supporting this male muscle power, masculine bones, heart and lungs are bigger and there is more haemoglobin in the blood. The female hand is only two-thirds as strong as that of the male.

The adult male body is also slightly larger than that of the female, the bigger skeleton providing a more powerful base for the increased muscle power. On average, the human male is 10 per cent heavier and 7 per cent taller than the human female. This means that, even when he does not deserve it, the human male will always have to be looked up to by the human female! For modern women seeking social equality this is one of the more irritating remnants of our ancient past, especially when we now live in a world where, thanks to modern technology, the brute strength required for hunting is of little importance to most people in ordinary day-to-day living.

Only on the sports field does superior male strength show itself in a significant way today. All over the world there are physical displays of male strength that help to emphasize the masculine advantage in this particular aspect of human biology. A dramatic example is to be seen each year in the traditional Highland Games in Scotland, where huge men compete in such bizarre events as tossing the caber. In this, a massive tree trunk from a fir or pine over 5 m (17 ft) long is tossed into the air. The competitor holds the trunk vertically, with the narrower end pressed against his chest, and then heaves it into the air so that it turns, end over end, falling to the ground with the narrower section pointing away from the thrower. Only the most powerful of men can achieve this feat, a feat which is beyond any woman.

Similar conspicuous demonstrations of masculine physical strength are found in many countries. Even on the notoriously relaxed islands of the South Pacific there is an

There is twice as much muscular tissue in the body of the human male, as in that of the human female. Dramatic reminders of this are the rituals of tossing the caber in the Scottish Highland Games (left) and the fruit-carrying contests of Polynesia (above).

annual fruit-carrying competition that tests the power of the local men in much the same way. In this display, a heavy pole laden with bunches of fruit weighing 45 kg (100 lb) has to be carried on one shoulder over a gruelling mile-long race, at the end of which the competitors collapse in agony as they cross the finishing line. The essence of such contests is that they should push the males concerned to the very limit of masculine strength, not only to discover which man is the strongest, but also to reaffirm the general superiority of male over female muscle.

Another physical difference between men and women also related to the hunting specialization of the human male is the shape of the face. Females have smaller noses, chins and jaws and thinner eyebrows than males, who are equipped with more prominent jaws, bigger noses and more powerful brows. This is because, when they set off on the hunt, males were in great physical danger. The heavier jaws and stronger brow-ridge acted as protection when grappling with prey, while the large nose improved the breathing efficiency of the male's larger lungs; lungs that had to assist his athletic pursuit of prey animals.

Proof of this facial divide between male and female is to be found in the E-Fit identification system used today by modern police forces. Their computerized system has two sets of features, one for each sex.

Women As Child-Bearers

Just as men have become anatomically improved as hunters, so women have become modified by virtue of their roles as child-bearers, food-gatherers and socially active organizers.

Again, this shows even at birth. The female baby is less vulnerable to disease than the male baby, and she retains this advantage throughout life. As a potential child-bearer she is reproductively less 'disposable' than the male and requires extra protection.

So, although females may not be as strong as males in a muscular sense, they are stronger in a medical sense. Not only do they suffer from fewer diseases and fewer accidents, they are also less likely to be stillborn or to suffer from physical deformity. They are less likely to suffer from colour-blindness – and the difference is enormous, with men being 75 times more likely to show this particular weakness. They are also less likely to suffer from acute depression and therefore less likely to commit suicide.

Other forms of 'extra protection' include a more generous layer of body fat. Females have twice as much fat as men – 25 per cent of their body weight, compared with only 12.5 per cent for males. This gives them a much greater resistance to famine and, therefore, a better chance of getting their infants through lean periods. Back in the days of hunting and gathering this was especially important because, at that stage, our ancestors had to face a feast-and-famine economy whenever they expanded into the less hospitable regions of the globe.

In addition to providing our female ancestors with an emergency food store, rather like a camel's hump, the extra fat also offered them improved insulation – much appreciated on cold nights or in freezing climates. Unlike the camel's hump, the human female's fat is spread over almost her entire body, which also gives her, incidentally, one of her most characteristic female gender signals – the curvaceousness of her body outline. Hence softly rounded curves became synonymous with female wellbeing and therefore with female sexuality.

(In ancient times, the high fat content of the human female body also had another, somewhat gruesome effect. According to the Greek historian Plutarch, 'Those whose business it is to burn bodies always add one woman to every 10 men. This helps the burning of bodies because the flesh of the woman is so fat that it burns like a torch.')

As regards their sense organs, female infants have better hearing, touch and smell than males. Again, these advantages last a lifetime. These are qualities that, as we shall see later, are of special benefit to the adult female when she becomes a mother. In their play, female infants show more caution and are more adept at activities involving sensitive manual dexterity. In their verbal skills girls are more fluent, while boys are more original. As with the studies of male infants, these findings support the idea of a deep-seated division of personality in our species, which, in turn, reflects the deep-rooted division of labour in our evolutionary past.

The child-bearing specialization of the human female has affected her adult body shape. Because women give birth between their legs, the female pelvic girdle is much broader than the male's and their legs are set wider apart. This influences female behaviour in several ways. They have a different style of walking, taking steps that are tiny compared with the long strides of the typical male. In many cultures, females who wish to emphasize their femininity have exaggerated this feature. To encourage this, they have often worn unusually tight skirts or precariously high heels. The abbreviated steps that then have to be taken create a super-female impression. The geishas of Kyoto in Japan, for example, have taken this trend to extremes and can be seen teetering along the streets of the city with minute, bird-like steps.

Evolution gave the primeval male hunter a longer stride that carried him further in his pursuit of game. And evolution gave the human female the best walk possible without damaging her ability to give birth. So, essentially, the female pelvic girdle is a compromise, performing two important tasks that make conflicting demands upon it. This inevitably limits the typical female's athletic ability, a fact that becomes particularly obvious in the running woman when she is observed from directly in front. The rotation of her legs is

The human female moves in a different way from the male, rotating her legs as she runs (left). Leg-crossing also differs between the sexes: both sexes show the ankle/ankle and the knee-knee cross (above centre and above right) but men are more likely to show the ankle/knee cross (above left), while only women perform the leg-twine (right).

immediately obvious, compared with the straight movement of the running male.

This strange, leg-swinging movement of the average female is easily overlooked because almost every time we do watch this particular activity it is being performed not by an average female but by a specially trained and selected female athlete. Those women who do become successful as athletes do so because they have an unusually masculine shape to their bodies, with narrow hips and a masculine gait. Watching the Olympic Games can give us a very distorted picture of the normal actions of the typical female body.

The shape of the human pelvis does not just influence the way we walk and run, but also the way we sit down. There are four different kinds of leg-crossing in the human species. Two of them are common to both sexes, one is typically male and one is essentially female. The most widespread is the knee-on-knee cross. This is done equally by both sexes, as is the more formal ankle-on-ankle. But the ankle-on-knee is predominantly male, even when women are wearing trousers. The fourth kind of leg-cross is the leg-twine, which is almost entirely female. In this the crossed-over foot is tucked round and behind the other leg. If men are asked to do this they find it extremely difficult and usually impossible. Some men refuse even to attempt this kind of leg-crossing when requested to do so, perhaps because they intuitively feel it is effeminate and will make them look foolish. This sex difference in leg-crossing is another example of the way in which the wide pelvis of the female has had an impact on other action-patterns.

The wider setting of the female legs has not only given them an extra form of leg-crossing, it has also enabled them to excel at the popular sport of horse-riding. Because the legs are set wider apart at the point where they meet the trunk the female rider has always had an advantage over her male companion. This advantage met a cruel blow in earlier centuries, however, when it was considered impolite for a woman to open her legs wide in public. This was because the open-leg posture was associated with the female position during copulation.

It was considered to be unladylike to display this position even when it was clearly linked to a non-sexual pursuit. A Byzantine historian made his feelings quite clear when he complained that women who ride like men were 'little better than whores'.

The solution for women who insisted on riding was a strange invention called the side-saddle. First introduced in the fifteenth century, this consisted of a normal saddle with the addition of two curved, leather-covered side-flanges or pommels. The female rider mounted the horse so that she sat sideways and then hooked her thighs over the two flanges which held her firmly in place. From a distance, with her riding-skirts spread out, she appeared to be perched precariously sideways on her horse and seemed to be in danger of slipping off if the animal began to gallop. She was in reality held firmly in place by the two hidden side-flanges, which she gripped between her clamped thighs.

The side-saddle went out of fashion in the 1930s, swept away in the rush to 'join the boys'. The new emancipated woman wanted to make a point, and riding like the men became a political statement. The situation remained unchanged until very recently, when some young women, now sufficiently confident in their independence, decided to return to the side-saddle posture. In Britain the Side-Saddle Association now has 1200 members, with more joining each year.

Genital Signals

The primary reproductive system of the human animal – the complex apparatus for producing eggs and sperm and for bringing them together   has the potential for being another major source of gender signals, but its impact is limited. In the female the genitals are, for the most part, housed internally and are therefore unavailable as a visual body display. This even applies to that small part of her reproductive system that is placed externally. When she stands naked, little is visible of her genital opening. It is effectively hidden by her pubic hair and by its secretive position, tucked up between her legs. Genitally speaking, her display is a negative one, signalling the absence of external protrusions.

For the adult male the matter is different. Although he lacks the highly conspicuous, brightly coloured external genitals of some of his monkey relatives, his large penis and pendulous testicles are nevertheless clearly visible, protruding through the bush of his pubic hair. The question arises as to whether this overt positioning of the male organs represents a positive gender display or whether it is purely mechanical. In other words, do the male genitals hang down between the legs as a way of saying, 'Look at me, I am a male', or simply because that is the best position for them in the anatomical scheme of things?

If one were designing a running, leaping, primeval hunter, the idea of placing testicles swinging loose between the legs would seem foolhardy, to say the least. Yet that is precisely what evolution has done. The vulnerability of these external genitals is such that there must be some powerful compensating advantage in placing them outside the body. Unless they are there purely as a visual male display, there must be a strong physiological benefit of some kind. The most widely stated explanation is that sperm production is more efficient at the lower temperature found outside the body wall. This is indeed true, because there is less oxygen available for the developing sperm at higher temperatures. Cooler testicles mean higher fertility – and it has been suggested that wearing tight jeans or other closely fitted trousers may cause falling sperm-counts by creating a 'hot zone'.

There is, however, a flaw in this argument. Zoologists who have looked at a number of

The side-saddle posture of the female rider (above) was developed as a way of avoiding the sexual signal transmitted by the 'spread-legs' posture.

The facial hair of the male (right) is a pure gender signal. Its evolution as a masculine display has made it possible to identify a human figure as an adult man even at a great distance.

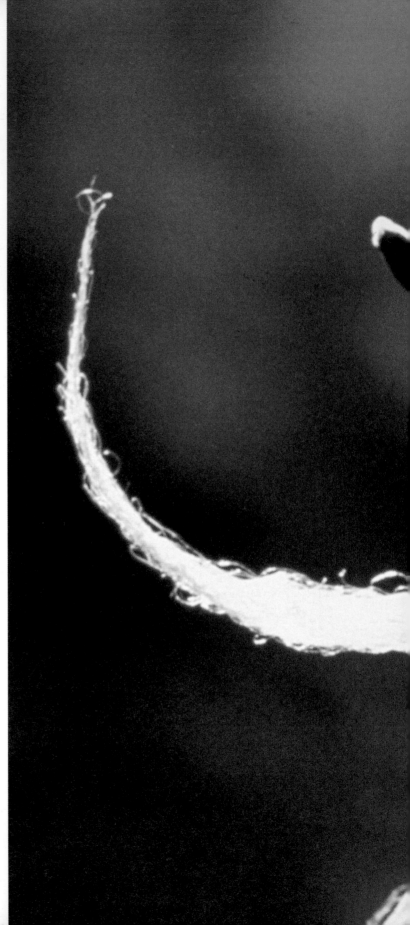

mammalian species have found that having external testicles does not always lead to a lowering of their temperature. So although cooling may be a secondary advantage, it cannot be the primary cause. This appears to be connected, not with temperature control, but with the type of locomotion an animal uses.

A recent survey of mammals with and without external testicles has shown that those species which have a 'jumping, leaping or galloping' lifestyle have external testicles. Those with a less 'concussive' type of movement keep their testicles safely tucked away inside their bodies. In other words, if you live a life of jolts and thuds, you cannot afford to keep your testicles inside your body wall because the pressures exerted on the internal organs during vigorous exercise would squeeze them so hard that their contents would be expelled. For example, with internal testicles, every time two rams head-butted one another, they would expel sperm. And every time a human hunter leapt down from a rock, he would do the same. This is because there is no sphincter on the reproductive tract. By placing the testicles outside the body, evolution has removed this pressure – an advantage apparently so great that it is worth risking the vulnerability of the exposed testicles.

This mechanical reason for the genital design of the human male would seem to provide a sufficient explanation for the visible position of the testicles. If this visibility then makes them available as a male gender signal, that is purely secondary.

The signal role of the penis is also secondary. This male appendage is easy to see because it is large, but its size is primarily concerned with its copulatory movements. It is long because this enables it to deposit sperm as far up the vagina as possible. And it is thick because this increases the 'massage' effect on the female sexual tissue, giving rise to female sexual arousal. This arousal leads to an intensification of the shared emotional experience of copulation and helps to cement the human pair-bond.

On the question of genital proportions, it should be mentioned that the size of the human testicles has also been the subject of some debate. Why are they the size they are, and why does the human male need to ejaculate over a hundred million sperm each time he reaches a sexual climax? An answer to this question was proposed in the 1980s when it was pointed out that different apes have different-sized testicles. The chimpanzee has very large testicles which are four times the weight of those belonging to the mighty gorilla, even though the gorilla's body weighs four times as much as that of the chimpanzee. It was also noted that chimpanzee females may mate with several chimpanzee males in quick succession, whereas there is little competition between gorilla males. From this it was concluded that, where female apes are promiscuous, the successful male needs to 'swamp out' the sperm of rival males. For this he requires a large ejaculate and that means large testicles.

Placed on this ape scale, the human animal has rather modest testicles – not quite as tiny as those of the gorilla, but much smaller than those of the chimpanzee. It suggests that, during the course of evolution, human males must have experienced only a moderate amount of sperm competition. This would fit with a picture of a species where the females are not promiscuous, but although typically faithful to one particular partner, may occasionally enjoy a little extra sexual activity with a second male – which is precisely what we find in human society. So testicle size, like the position of the testicles, is more a matter of mechanics than of display.

To sum up, although it is possible to identify the sex of a naked adult human simply by looking at the pubic region, there is nothing about the appearance of the external genitals that has been specially evolved as a visual signal. They have not become elaborately ornamented or brightly coloured as they have in some other species. What one sees is simply what is necessary for the mechanics of successful human copulation.

Pure Gender Signals

In addition to gender differences that arise as a secondary factor there are also some primary gender identification signals that have evolved to that end alone. Broad shoulders in a male may act as a gender signal, but their primary role is connected with the need for greater muscular strength. The wider hips of the female may give a silhouette that spells out 'feminine', but their primary function is connected with the private act of giving birth. The division of labour creates differences which, in turn, become visible gender 'labels', but they do not start out that way. Others, however, do.

Male facial hair has no function other than as a gender display. It makes it possible to identify the sex of an individual even from a great distance. If it is left untouched and remains undamaged it will grow to an amazing length. The record for a male moustache is 339 cm (just over 11 ft). The owner of this remarkable display is an Indian by the name of Kalyan Ramji Sain from the town of Sundargarth, who carefully protected his hairy outgrowth for 20 years before winning his place in the *Guinness Book of Records*. The longest beard in the world, now in the Smithsonian Institute in Washington, was owned by a Norwegian called Hans Langseth. Even longer than the record moustache, it measured no less than 533 cm (17.5 ft).

The absence of a beard in male children confirms that this appendage is, essentially, a sexual display. After puberty the unshaven beard grows at a rate of approximately 6 in (15 cm) a year. This means that, untrimmed, it would reach down to his navel in only three or four years. In the naked, primeval condition this must have presented an extraordinary sight, rivalling the dark mane of an adult male lion in terms of dramatic visual impact. No other biological feature would make the human male look more different from the human female.

The human female breast is also an important sexual signal. It has been wrongly stated in the past that it is no more than a milk-producing device and that male interest in it is infantile. This is incorrect because only one-third of the tissue of the breast is concerned with milk production. Two-thirds of it is simply fatty tissue, which gives it its shape but has nothing to do with milk production. And it is the rounded shape that is the important sexual signal. A lactating female chimpanzee has a rounded breast, but when she is not giving milk she has a flat chest. That does not happen with the adult human female. She retains the rounded shape to her breast throughout her fecundity period – that is to say, from the period of puberty until she reaches old age. The hemispherical shape of the human breast therefore has nothing to do with maternal behaviour and everything to do with sexual signalling. (In terms of sexual signalling, the covering of the breasts is the female equivalent of male beard-shaving – they both reduce the visual impact of the primeval gender signal.)

The sexual nature of the protruding female breast has given rise to a small male–female difference in body language of which most people are unaware. Unconsciously, the female uses a different action when she squeezes past another person in a narrow space. Males turn their chests towards the other person, but females nearly always turn away, protecting their vulnerable breasts from contact. The male action enables him to keep an eye on the person he is passing, and this serves to protect him from any sudden attack. The female

The rounded shape of the female breast is sexual rather than maternal. Only one-third of the breast tissue is concerned with milk production.
Lap-dancing at a British night-club (left).
Public breast-display at the New Orleans Mardi Gras (below).

could also benefit in this way, but chooses instead the more risky alternative of turning her back rather than appear to be presenting her breasts to the person who is squeezing past her.

Vocal Contrasts

One biological difference between men and women that is so obvious we take it for granted is the depth of the adult voice. At puberty, the voices of boys break and rapidly deepen. The voices of girls retain the higher pitch of childhood throughout the adult life span.

The details are as follows: the male larynx is one-third larger than the female larynx. Male vocal cords are 18 mm (0.7 in) long; female cords only 13mm (0.5 in). The adult male voice averages 130-145 cycles per second; the adult female voice, 230-255 cycles, one octave higher. The difference in pitch between the male and female laugh is even greater.

The difference between the male and female adult voice is greater than that heard in our closest relatives, the great apes. So why the increased contrast? There are two separate questions to be answered here: why do men gain a deeper voice, and why do women not do so?

The deeper masculine voice gives the adult male a more frightening roar, snarl and shout. This can be used to intimidate human rivals, to drive prey or to scare off predators. When human males first began eating meat, before they became full-time hunters, they probably began by scavenging – by getting together to drive off large carnivores from their freshly killed prey. This required great courage and active co-operation and they would certainly have benefited from a deeper roar to frighten away their powerful rivals.

The higher feminine voice gives the adult female a more juvenile quality. Along with several other features, such as less hairy body skin, the high voice of the adult female transmits signals to the male that make him feel more protective. By sounding like a little child the female can arouse the caring, paternal feelings of her mate and, in this way, improve her chances of survival when rearing his children.

Fiercely independent modern females may see this interpretation of their high-pitched voices as insulting but the fact remains that the primeval female, with her heavy parental burden, needed all the help she could get to protect herself and her offspring. If she could do this by employing juvenile characteristics then evolution would be quick to give her this advantage.

In the modern world this ancient strategy can sometimes misfire. What works well enough inside the family can be exploited in the office. Because of its juvenile and therefore essentially subordinate quality, the higher pitch of the female voice can be used deliberately by dominant males to make them feel superior. According to a recent report, female employees in some Japanese companies 'are expected to wear prissy matching uniforms and speak in tones high enough to shatter the office window-panes – a classic form of female deference in Japan'.

By encouraging a small, squeaky voice, the male bosses make it difficult for female statements or opinions to carry any weight. It follows that the opposite trend could favour females in the corridors of power and it is rumoured that, in the West, some top female politicians have employed private voice coaches to help them deepen their tones in order to add authority to their pronouncements.

Mental Differences

The physical differences between men and women are beyond question. The facts are there for all to see (or hear). But what of mental differences? Here the matter becomes immediately controversial. Mental activity is so strongly influenced by learning and training that any suggestion about differences in 'male thinking' or 'female thinking', 'male intelligence' or 'female intelligence' is instantly condemned as old-fashioned, bigoted and sexist. This has become a dangerous area to discuss, but, as a scientist, if I allow fashionable taboos to stop me from asking objective questions, I am lost. If there is a possibility that there might be mental differences between men and women, then it is important to face up to these and take them into account, rather than attempt to sweep them under a politically correct carpet. If they exist and they are ignored it will, in the end, do nobody any favours.

What are the chances that male and female brains do work in a slightly different way? We know there was a primeval division of labour between the sexes and that this led to a slight degree of physical specialization, so it seems

Co-operative male hunting : prehistoric cave art at Niaux in Southern France, showing a bison pierced with arrows.

(next page)

reasonable to assume that there was an accompanying degree of mental specialization as well. The different preoccupations of prehistoric males and females would have benefited from a bias towards slightly different mental processes. Male hunters, for example, were required to focus on persistent, prolonged pursuits and to concentrate on long-term goals. They had to be good at dwelling on a single, central problem to the exclusion of other side issues. To be good on the hunt they had to become slightly more single-minded than their female companions.

In addition, the males had to improve their visual and spatial skills, becoming better at trekking and planning, tracking and aiming, searching and homing. Also, they had to become adept at the technology of weapon-making – at manufacturing, maintaining, repairing and improving their implements. Finally, they had to be prepared to take risks. In terms of breeding units men have always been more expendable than women, and if one gender had to take risks it would have to be the male.

The primitive females, by contrast, had to be especially good at thinking of many things at once, and at organizing them all simultaneously. Gathering food did not require single-minded concentration, but it did demand social organization and communication. And, since prehistoric women were very much at the centre of society, while their men were away hunting in remote places they had to be efficient at running social affairs, controlling the business of the camp site and discussing the details of community life.

As someone once said, 'Women are interested in people, men in things'. Although this is a caricature of the truth, it is nevertheless based on a genuine and important difference, one that, from primeval times, has led men to become interested in technology and women in social skills. As a result, any visit today to a collectors' exhibition or model-builders' convention will reveal a predominantly male audience. Any gathering of social workers, charity organizers or other caring activities will be predominantly female.

In addition to being more fluent, primitive females would also have been more cautious. They could not afford to take serious risks because they were too important to the reproductive success of the tribe and because they had to protect themselves as best they could to be available for caring for their babies.

In a nutshell, the women had to become fine-tuned as careful communicators and organizers, capable of doing several things at once without becoming confused. If men had to improve their single-minded concentration, their visual skills and their sometimes rash bravery, women had to become better at multi-directional thinking, verbal skills and common-sense caution.

What evidence can we find today that supports the idea that modern men and women are still subject to this biological division of 'mental labour'? Unfortunately, because we live in societies where for centuries women have been unfairly subordinated to men, it is hard to separate the biological from the cultural. In order to do this, it is necessary to find areas where culture does not seem to be interfering, and where the two sexes are genuinely given equal opportunity. Only then can we be sure that observed differences in success rate have any underlying biological meaning.

One way to do this is to study the differences between male and female newborn infants, before adults have had time to influence the way they behave. As already mentioned, there are several key differences, even at this tender age. In infant play, males are more percussive, girls more dextrous. Boy babies are more exploratory; girls more cautious. Boys are better at visual/spatial tasks; girls at verbal/communicatory tasks.

Among adults it is more difficult to avoid cultural bias. Perhaps the easiest area to study is risk-taking, and here there really does appear to be a significant biological difference between the sexes. Throughout life women are less likely than men to die of a violent accident. By the age of 30, in some countries, males are 15 times more likely to die of an accident than women. A recent study of road accidents, for example, has shown that, although women drivers may have more mishaps than men, when men are involved the insurance claims are much heavier. In other words, men have fewer minor crashes, but a greater number of serious ones.

A simple experiment can verify this. If men and women are asked to try their hand at go-karting for the first time, their different mental approach is immediately obvious. The women are more tentative and, although travelling at reasonable speeds, do their best to keep their karts on the road. The men, despite their inexperience, drive as fast as they possibly can and, as a result, repeatedly crash into the barriers.

An unexpected way in which risk-taking differences surface today concerns the response of males and female to spiders. There is a common fear of spiders which can

The bicycle test: ask a man and a woman to draw a bicycle from memory, and the woman (above) finds it much harder than the man (below).

be observed in both sexes – recent tests have shown that spider-hatred is second only to snake-hatred. For our ancient ancestors this was a valuable reaction because there were indeed some dangerous spiders that could have harmed them. Today, in Britain, where spider-reaction tests were carried out, there are no dangerous species at all, so the reaction we are witnessing must have survived from ancient times. Intriguingly, the strength of the response is not the same for males and females. At puberty, the female hatred dramatically increases until it is twice as strong as that of the male. Rather than indicating a weakness in the young female, this suggests a greater need for her to protect herself at the moment when, in a primitive society, she is liable to start breeding. It is a sign of the greater caution shown by the female – a caution that was appropriate in ancient times, considering her procreative value to the tribe.

At about the same age the love of some animals, such as horses, shows a dramatic increase in pre-pubertal girls, but not in boys. A careful investigation revealed that, at its peak, just before the teenage phase, the love of horses rises to become three times stronger in girls compared with boys. This suggests a difference in the psychology of young girls, with greater emphasis on an attachment to larger, more powerful companions. But if the horse symbolizes a male force to which they turn, it should not be forgotten that it is they, the small girls, who ultimately control the horses.

What of the difference between visual and verbal skills? It is common knowledge that, faced with a difficult problem, men are likely to go off and ponder it silently while women get together and talk it out. Men may be good at public speaking, but women are far better at discussing. In general, women seem to be better at languages, while men are stronger in technological subjects.

A simple test can demonstrate this. Both men and women know perfectly well what a bicycle looks like and both sexes ride them in large numbers. But if men and women are presented with a piece of paper on which two equal circles are drawn side by side, representing the wheels of a bicycle, and asked to complete the drawing, the men fare much better than the women.

The evidence for superior female verbal abilities is overwhelming. For example, many verbal difficulties that adults face are predominantly masculine. Stuttering, which has been defined as 'a disability in the production of fluent speech', is four times more common in men than in women. The severe reading disability known as dyslexia is also predominantly a male phenomenon. Mild dyslexia is five times more common in males; severe dyslexia is 10 times more common. Males also suffer greater language impairment and recover language abilities much more slowly following strokes or other forms of brain damage.

Female superiority in verbal abilities starts early in life. Even in the womb, a difference has been detected between the mouth movements of male and female foetuses. A medical research team working in Belfast recently discovered that, between the ages of 8 and 20 weeks' gestation, female foetuses 'exhibit more frequent and longer bouts of mouth movements than males'. Interestingly, male foetuses showed more powerful and more frequent limb movements than females. In other words, even before they are born, human females show signs that they will become better talkers and the males give indications that they will become better athletes.

After they have been born, the same trend continues. Little girls aged between one and five years are more advanced in word usage than their male counterparts. Girls talk sooner than boys and make use of longer phrases when speaking. They also make more varied word constructions, make fewer verbal errors and have a larger vocabulary than small boys of the same age. All through the school years, girls show better word use, with superior spelling skills, punctuation and reading ability. In careful tests carried out with schoolchildren, it emerged that two-thirds of the top marks in language tests were obtained by girls. The researchers involved emphasize that it is in *quality* of word use rather than quantity that girls excel.

New research from the Johns Hopkins University in Baltimore has added further support to the idea of female supremacy in the sphere of verbal fluency. It has been discovered that, in the region of the cortex concerned with this ability, the female brain has a greater concentration of cells. In the area dealing with verbal initiative and short-term memory, women show a 23 per cent higher concentration, and in the area linked to listening skills it was nearly 13 per cent higher. This provides strong evidence for the anatomical basis of the gender differences in verbal abilities.

The evidence for superior male visual abilities is equally impressive. Visual-spatial skills are especially important in the spheres of engineering, architecture, building and aviation, and it is not surprising to find that these activities are largely male-dominated. In careful tests males scored higher in solving maze-problems, map-reading, perspectives, geometry, architectural plans, spatial perception and object rotation. Sometimes the contrast between the sexes is only slight, but occasionally there are dramatic differences. In a simple water-level test, for example, where students were asked to guess the position of the water surface in a tilted glass, girls failed more than twice as often as boys. The test seemed easy enough – would the student realize that the water level stayed horizontal even when the glass containing the liquid was tipped further on its side? Despite this, the difference between the sexes was remarkable.

The consequences of these gender differences in verbal and visual abilities should be that some occupations are male-dominated and others are female-dominated. Supporting this is a survey carried out in Sweden. There, more than a decade after the introduction of a strict code of sexual equality, the career choices of male and female schoolchildren remained markedly different from one another. Technical careers were predominantly male and social careers largely female. The percentages are dramatic: categories listed as building, construction, technology, workshop, woodwork and motor engineering attracted 94 per cent to 98 per cent male applicants; categories listed as social services, consumer studies and nursing and care attracted 92 per cent to 97 per cent female applicants.

It is impossible to explain such a vast difference simply on the basis of cultural pressure, because there was no cultural pressure at that moment in Swedish history. In fact, one might have predicted a swing the other way. With the escape from sexual bias to formally imposed sexual equality one might have expected to see a rebellion against career-bias, with the schoolchildren striking a blow for freedom by deliberately making a switch. But instead they retained as great a bias as ever.

To sum up, there are some mental tasks for which men are intrinsically better suited and some for which women are better suited. To ignore this because of a fashionable myth that it is sexist even to hint at such differences is to do a serious disservice to both sexes.

The reason why mental differences between the sexes has been such a sensitive area in recent years is because of the fear that there will be a risk of over-simplifying and labelling one sex as generally more intelligent than the other. This is clearly not the case, but there is one intriguing difference that has been suggested which does apply to general intelligence rather than to specifics. This concerns the frequency of genius individuals.

It has been claimed that, in the past, individuals usually accepted as being at the highest genius level have nearly always been male. That this does not stem merely from male dominance. The argument runs that, to succeed at the highest level, the individual must be obsessional almost to the point of madness and must be able to ignore all the social and family distractions that most ordinary people find it impossible to avoid. Geniuses tend to live chaotic, troubled lives in which their immense talents lead them into all kinds of social and emotional difficulties and often involve them in high dramas. The male lifestyle favours this type of essentially selfish behaviour more than the female's. Also, genius flies in the face of common sense and the ability to deal with many things at once, which are strong female qualities. The genius must be single-minded beyond reason, and this is more suited to the typical male personality.

Developing this theme, it has been suggested that, if one looks at general levels of intelligence in large numbers of adults, there is a characteristic male and female pattern. As with special skills, there is not one 'superior' sex and one 'inferior' sex. Instead, there is a different kind of frequency distribution. The male 'intelligence curve' is wider and shallower than that of the female. This means that, not only will there be more male geniuses, but there will also be – at the other end of the curve – more male morons. The female curve is narrower and taller. In other words, if intelligence is divided into three levels, genius/intelligent/stupid, there will be more males at the two extremes but more females in the middle, at the intelligent level.

It is hard to see how this argument can be verified scientifically because there are too many subjective elements involved. However, one attempt to do so was carried out by a Cambridge don, Charles Goodhart, who analysed the examination results of large numbers of male and female undergraduates. He found that, 'Men get many more first-class degrees – and thirds and failures. The women are bunched in the middle. They almost all get 2.1s or 2.2s – fewer very bright ones, but fewer stupid ones either.'

His comments brought howls of protest, but he backed them up by pointing out that, genetically, it makes sense: females have two X chromosomes, while males have one X and one Y, leading to greater variability. And he suggested that this rule would apply to other qualities as well. Men, for example, should show a greater variability in body height – and indeed they do: 'You get very tall men and very short men; but women are much more of a muchness'.

It has to be said that greater mental variability in men would also make sense in evolutionary terms. Females were too valuable reproductively to take any risks with, so they stayed safely 'intelligent', thereby increasing the safety of their children. Males, on the other hand, were reproductively more disposable, so it made genetic sense to 'experiment' with them, maintaining a high scatter of mental types. This ensured the repeated arrival of eccentric, exceptional or unusual male brains that kept up the creative pressure and, once in a while, came up with a major innovation that thrust the human species a little further forward. If, in the process, some of these 'experiments' misfired and the geniuses went mad, little was lost in the overall reproductive picture.

This division of mental labour, if it truly exists at a biological level, would be an efficient way of *safely* rearing one's offspring and *unsafely* inventing the future, at one and the same time.

Different But Equal

These then are some of the major biological differences between men and women. Some are direct sexual signals identifying males as males and females as females. Others can be explained by referring back to the primeval division of labour that developed in our species, with the hunting males being designed for speed and strength and the food-gathering, child-bearing females characterized by stamina and maternity. Combined together these varying pressures have moulded our bodies and created the adult human male and the adult human female forms as they are today in all their subtle splendour.

2

Language of the Sexes

Every human male and human female has an efficient set of biological gender signals, but the cultures in which they live cannot leave these alone. They modify them in a thousand different ways, exaggerating some and suppressing others, changing them and making them more and more elaborate, translating the biological language of the sexes into a cultural babel.

Today, when human beings display their genders, instead of quietly transmitting their basic reproductive signals they noisily proclaim their adult status with all the complexity that modern life can offer them. We have grown accustomed to this and have fine-tuned ourselves to respond to the latest beauty fashions with all the subtle details of make-up, hairstyling and clothing. When looking for a partner we take into account a thousand tiny details of cosmetics, costumes and other visual elements. The amazing computers inside our skulls perform lightning calculations every time we set eyes on an attractive member of the opposite sex, instantly assessing their partner appeal. If someone scores a perfect 'ten', we know this immediately, but if we were asked to analyse the separate factors involved, we would find it extremely difficult because our assessment is based on such a long and complicated set of cultural influences.

Sex and Beauty

Why have we made pairing so hard for ourselves? If a member of the opposite sex has the basic gender signals, the basic physical properties and reasonable intelligence, what is to stop us pairing off with them? The answer lies in what has been called 'the beauty trap'. We have applied a whole series of sophisticated standards to what we consider to be a suitable mate for ourselves in our modern social context. We may not be aware of the way we have done this – it is simply what is 'in vogue' or 'on our wavelength'. We are caught inside the strands of the cultural web which the spider of social custom weaves around each one of us from the time we are born. And to make matters even more complicated, this differs in detail for each of our societies.

Every human society has its own special standards of beauty. When a careful study was made in 200 different cultures to find out what was especially appealing, there were hardly any qualities that were found everywhere. Many of the obvious sexual signals were not as universally accepted as previously believed.

For every culture that favoured large female breasts, another liked small ones. If one culture liked white teeth, another preferred black teeth or filed-down teeth. If one liked long, flowing hair, another insisted on shaved heads. If one liked skinny bodies, another preferred fat ones, and so on. Sometimes the preferences were almost arbitrary, or based simply on the *opposite* of the tribe next door, to create a distinctive difference. More often than not, they were exaggerations of one or other of the many human gender signals. What made them different was that one culture would focus on, say, the lips, while another would concentrate on the neck or the feet. In each case they would take a particular feature and then push it to extremes. They were in the business of creating what has been called 'super-normal stimuli'.

Nothing could be more super-normal than the amazing lip-plates worn by certain African tribeswomen. If it is sexy for a woman to have large fleshy lips, then why not make them even bigger? Cut a slit in them when she is young and push a small plate into them to stretch them out. Then, as she grows older, replace the plate with a bigger one and keep making them bigger until she ends up with super-lips that should, in theory, be super-sexy. Usually the first plates are only coin-sized, but they eventually become large enough to serve a meal on. In some tribes there are even double plates, one for the upper lip as well as for the lower, which makes eating, drinking and smoking extremely difficult. What it does for sexual foreplay has not been recorded.

In the Surma and Mursi tribes of Ethiopia the lip-plates of the women are so important as ways of making the young women sexually attractive that the bride price will be determined by the size of the plate. The bigger the plate of an unmarried girl, the more she is worth, the largest plates of all fetching 50 head of cattle, a fortune in local terms. Needless to say, this stretches the elasticity of human flesh almost to breaking point. Local rules allow that the lip-plates can only be removed when in the company of other women, when eating in private, or when sleeping, but they must always be worn when in the company of men.

If large female lips (right) are
sexy, then some cultures will
exaggerate them (above) as a
special sign of beauty. If female
necks are long and slender
(opposite page, left), then other
cultures will exaggerate those
features, too (opposite page,
right), as a beauty display.

Amazingly, this particular facial improvement which, to Western eyes, looks so much like a facial deformity, has developed independently in several different cultures as far apart as tropical Africa and the forests of South America. We may find it bizarre, but it is worth remembering that, in a very modest way, our own culture employs a similar lip exaggeration. Women frequently make their lips look a little larger by painting them with bright lipstick and allowing the painted edge to stray outside the real edge of the lips. This fashion was introduced by prostitutes in ancient Egypt to make themselves more appealing to their customers and has since spread to become a major industry. More recently, collagen or fat implants have been used to produce permanently swollen 'bee-sting' lips. So the difference between the 'deformity' of lip-plates and the 'beautifying' of Western lips is only a matter of degree. In both cases there is an exaggeration of a female sexual response – the response that sees a marked swelling of the lips during intense sexual arousal. Culture extends what nature intends.

A similar process is at work in other regions of the body. The female neck is longer and more slender than that of the male. It follows that, if something can be done to make

43

the female neck look even longer and thinner, this will increase the femininity of the gender display. The most extraordinary example of this is to be found among the amazing giraffe-necked women of Burma. These remarkable women, from the Padaung sub-group of the Karen people from eastern Burma's Kayah state, start putting brass rings around their necks when they are very young. As they grow they add more and more rings which push their shoulders down further and further. This gives the impression that they have immensely long necks. The goal is to reach the maximum number of rings, which for some reason is generally agreed to be 32.

The origin of the neck-rings is said to date back to a time when the women were threatened by a tiger that would bite their necks and kill them. The rings were thought to provide adequate protection against these attacks. Younger Padaung women give a simpler explanation for their strange custom: 'Wearing brass rings around your neck makes you beautiful'. The problem for these women is not, as one might think, a practical one of how to keep active, but how to find the money to pay for the expensive rings. Their solution in recent years has been to move across the border into Thailand where they can sell themselves to be photographed by tourists at $10 a time. To some this is deplorable as an example of ethnic exploitation, but it does at least keep the ancient tradition alive.

Another female feature that can be singled out for cultural emphasis is the wider hip. In West Africa, Cameroon women take special care to pad out their skirts to give the impression that their hips are even wider – and therefore more child-bearing – than they already are. In Western cultures, a slimmer, more juvenile silhouette is generally preferred, now that breeding has been dramatically slowed down, but in the Cameroon, where the breeding rate is 4 times higher than in Europe, maternal signals are still given precedence over juvenile ones.

In the Western world, generous hips may not be so popular but generous breasts are still in favour. Because the hemispherical shape of the female breast is such a powerful sexual signal for our species, it is not surprising to find that some cultures take steps to enhance this feature of the body. In the United States, in particular, breast implants have become immensely popular with show girls. The effect is to create breasts that are firm and almost rigidly rounded, no matter what actions their owners perform. This creates a powerful visual image but whether these improved breasts *feel* sexual is another matter.

In the context of a sex club, however, this is of little importance because touching is strictly taboo.

Throughout history different cultures have selected different aspects of the body for exaggeration. In China it used to be the custom to improve on nature by exaggerating the smallness of the female foot. Excruciatingly painful foot-binding was started in childhood. Mothers would demand that their daughters, from the age of seven, would bind their little feet with a special bandage, 5 cm (2 in) wide and 3 m (10 ft) long, curling the smaller toes tightly back and under, leaving only the big toe free. As the bandage wound tighter and tighter, it also pulled the sole of the foot closer and closer to the heel. After several years of this treatment, the feet became permanently deformed, crushed up and stumpy, almost like a little hoof. They would then fit inside the tiny, exquisitely embroidered shoes that were made for ladies of high status which were only a few inches long.

The minute, hoof-like foot, known as the Golden Lotus, was seen by Chinese men as the height of erotic beauty. During lovemaking they would caress the Golden Lotus, suck it, nibble it and even take it completely into the mouth. It became the focus of erotic longing. Because women have smaller feet than men it followed that to exaggerate this difference created a super-feminine female. Only peasants had flat feet, or 'duck feet' as they were scathingly called. (And it is not surprising to learn that the story of Cinderella – whose ugly sisters failed to squeeze their large feet into her tiny shoe – originated in China.)

The custom of Chinese foot-binding lasted nearly a thousand years, from the tenth century to the beginning of the twentieth, when it was at last put a stop to as cruel and barbaric. Its persistence over such a long period was due to a double significance, for the foot not only acted as an erotic zone, but also became a badge of high status. This was because no woman with bound feet could ever perform manual labour. To walk on a pair of Golden Lotuses meant an entire life of courtly restraint, enforced inactivity and fidelity.

We may raise our hands in horror at the idea of crippling young girls in that way, but we ourselves have not been completely immune from this type of exaggeration. The well-heeled Western shoe, although a pale shadow of the Chinese footwear, is nevertheless a gross distortion of what nature intended. Like the Chinese shoes, the Western high-heeled shoes incapacitate the wearers. They are far less extreme, of course, but they still

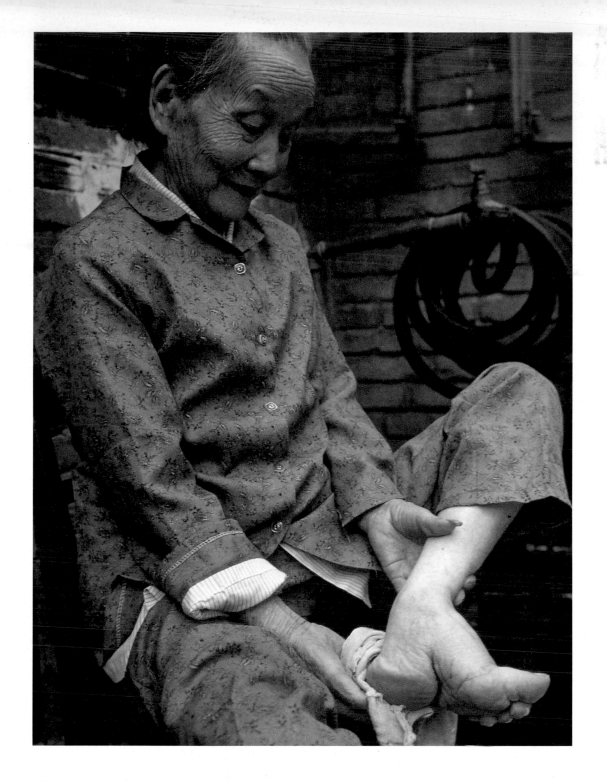

The movements of the traditional belly-dance (left) exaggerate the wider hips of the female figure. For centuries, Chinese foot-binding (above) helped to exaggerate the smaller size of the female foot.

make the wearer look more delicate, more vulnerable and therefore more likely to arouse the protective instincts of the human male. As with the lip exaggerations, it is only a matter of degree. The principle is just the same. (Interestingly, a larger female foot is regarded as a sexual turn-off to such an extent that a whole song has been written on the subject – Fats Waller's 'Your Feet's Too Big!' – which ends with the famous line: 'Your pedal extremities are obnoxious'.)

Whether we like it or not, individual beauty now plays a vital role in mate selection. And, in a strange way, it has lost its primeval common sense. Today, a woman with a stunningly beautiful face will be more appealing as a potential mate than one with a plain face, regardless of her maternal qualities. Even if she has narrow hips, is barren, bad-tempered and vain, an exquisitely beautiful woman will still be able to compete for a mate with a homely, but otherwise highly compatible and fertile rival. The same is true for the male sex. A handsome man with a hugely dubious personality will always be able to compete with a plain man who is loyal and kind. (And this extends beyond mate selection into the more general world of employment and staff selection. One recent survey revealed that 'beautiful people' on average earn five per cent more than their plainer counterparts. Another investigation put the figure as high as 12 per cent.)

In other words, status is given precedence over breeding. In any other species this bizarre situation would be unthinkable, but in our over-crowded human communities the emphasis on breeding potential has dwindled and the desire for a public status display has risen. In the complex social hierarchy of today, it is the sexual companion capable of making rivals envious that is preferred over the one who promises to be an ideal breeding partner. This shift is one of the main complicating factors in modern mate selection. The young adult not only has to find a mate, but also has to find one who satisfies special, almost unattainable qualities of physical glamour.

It is little wonder that there has been a recent rebellion against this new tyranny. Unfortunately this rebellion has been rather one-sided and has been made a feminist issue rather than a more general, human one. American author Naomi Wolf comments, 'There is no…biological justification for the beauty myth; what it is doing to women today is a result of nothing more exalted than the need of today's power structure, economy and culture to mount a counteroffensive against women…The beauty myth is not about women at all. It is about men's institutions and institutional power.'

Her criticism of the beauty myth is absolutely correct, but her explanation of what lies behind it is strongly reminiscent of what someone referred to as 'campaign gibberish'. To suggest that concepts of beauty derive from some kind of male plot against women overlooks two important points. First, male appearance is just as much a part of the myth as female beauty. Is this a female plot against men? Secondly, the female beauty myth is kept alive as much by women as it is by men. This is not a battle to be fought in the gender wars, it is a matter of concern for both sexes.

Having said this, it must be admitted that the situation is not quite as simple as it may first appear. On closer examination it emerges that there are two relevant kinds of beauty. The first has to do with the subtle local nuances of what makes the sexiest, most glamorous face, be it male or female. These will vary from place to place and also from time to time, as role models and fashionable idols change. This is the film-star beauty, the model-girl glamour, the mystique of the handsome male hunk. It is the kind of perfectionist beauty that has more to do with sculptural aesthetics and hero/heroine worship than with genuine, down-to-earth mate selection. This is the competitive, high stakes beauty that has invaded family life and made a mockery of reproductive biology.

Quite distinct from that form of artificially refined – and highly variable – beauty is a more universal set of key elements of human visual appeal. Together these constitute what might be termed 'biological beauty'. The key elements are: (1) the basic gender signals (broad male shoulders, wide female hips etc.); (2) signs of youthfulness (vigour, flexibility, bounciness, smooth body surfaces); (3) signs of health (clear skin, lack of disease, physical fitness); and (4) symmetrical features.

These are the only visual elements that have the same appeal in all cultures. Other details, such as the shape of the nose, the length of the hair and the size of the breasts, vary from society to society and tribe to tribe. The first three all make good sense in terms of fitness to breed and it is easy to see why these are all immediately attractive to the opposite sex. The fourth is rather more mysterious and needs some explanation.

Studies of 'symmetry appeal' are quite recent and have thrown up some unexpected results. Tests with pictures of human faces showing different degrees of asymmetry have revealed that the more symmetry there is in a face, the more appealing it is considered to be. Careful measurements of 72 volunteers showed that the smallest degree of asymmetry (one to two per cent) was thought to be the most appealing; a higher degree (five to seven per cent) the least appealing. Furthermore, the most symmetrical individuals enjoyed a better sex life. Symmetrical men, on average, started their sex lives three to four years earlier than more lopsided men. And the female partners of symmetrical men enjoyed orgasms in 75 per cent of sexual incidents, compared with only 30 per cent for lopsided men. Also, simultaneous orgasms were more common for the more symmetrical individuals.

There is much argument about why body symmetry should be so sexy. The answer seems to lie in the realm of health. From animal studies we know that diseased mothers give birth to offspring that show greater asymmetries. Animals that suffer from inbreeding also give birth to offspring with greater asymmetry. From human studies, we know that women with asymmetrical breasts are less fertile than those with greater symmetry. It would appear that, during the process of growth, both before and after birth, symmetrical individuals are fitter, stronger and healthier, with more efficient immune systems. So it makes good evolutionary sense if such individuals are seen as more appealing. The reaction to them is not, of course, analysed as it happens. Nobody is consciously aware of how they are reacting; it is a secret subtext in the body language of sexual encounters.

Combined together, these universals of youth, health and symmetry give a basic form of biological beauty that is recognized across cultures in a remarkable way. For example, when women from England, China and India were shown photographs of Greek men and asked to rate them for appeal, they all gave the same answers. Other similar tests involving as many as 13 different cultures produced the same results.

Perhaps the most significant findings came from tests done with babies. When infants only a few months old were shown pairs of photographs of adult faces they gazed much longer at those that had been independently judged by adults to be the most attractive. This supports the idea of the existence of a universal beauty factor in human appearance long before any cultural influences can have started to operate.

So it would seem that we have to accept the existence of

Play-fighting: young lovers often behave in a juvenile way, unconsciously amplifying their signals of youthfulness, signals that have universal sex appeal.

two layers of beauty: a universal layer that enables us to judge the physical appeal of someone from the other side of the world, belonging to a different race, and a localized, cultural layer that varies according to a whole set of almost arbitrary fashion rules. The first gives us our common humanity; the second our rich variety of cultures.

Signs of Youth

One of the features mentioned above that has universal appeal is youthfulness. It is a sobering fact, as we grow older, that where sexuality is concerned the younger a human adult is, the stronger are the sexual signals that he or she transmits. The focus of this sexuality is in the skin tone and the muscle tone. Smooth skin, a flexible torso and lithe

limbs all contribute to create a powerful image of sex appeal. The young leap and bounce where their elders plod or droop. The bodies of the young seem strangely softer and lighter, as though the force of gravity is being unfairly kind to them. These are powerful sexual features that never fail to impress the eyes of the beholder.

For young females, the youthful opposition to the force of gravity is especially relevant in one particular part of their bodies. Their breasts lack any kind of sag. As females grow older this sag increases until, in very old age, the breasts have finally drooped flat on their chests. There is one important stage when, at the end of the teenage phase, in the early 20s, the breasts have become fully swollen but have not yet started to sag. This is the time when they have maximum sex appeal and it is no accident that this is also the time when the human female is most ready, in other respects, to breed. (The age of maximum fecundity for the human female – that is, the age at which she is most likely to be success-ful at bringing her foetus to term – is 22.) The pert breasts of the female on the threshold of adulthood are a special signal to the male, a sexual display that he finds irresistible.

The fact that this youthful 'anti-gravity' display will never be as strong again has been the cause of consternation to many women and has given rise to the invention of the tight bodice, the bra and, more recently, the silicone implant. All these devices are attempts to transmit false signals of youthfulness from older female chests. Their widespread popularity underlines the potency of youthfulness as a sexual signal.

As the muscle tone of the body declines with advancing years, other parts of the body also benefit from a little artificial help. As with the breasts, the fatty tissue of the buttocks sags more as their owners grow older. Tight jeans or trousers help to correct this and in recent years special garments have been marketed to appeal to those who wish to present a more youthful rear to admiring eyes. These include, in all seriousness, products with names such as the 'Bum-bra', the 'Bottombra', 'Bottom Falsies' and 'Miracle Boost Denims'. The designers of these inventions employ the latest fabric technology to lift, firm and protrude the buttocks. Appealing as this may be, the problem with such devices is that they only work as long as the body transmitting the youthful signals remains fully clothed. If the sexual display is successful and leads to more intimate encounters, the moment will arrive when the body is naked and the artificial firmness of counterfeit youth must give way to the flabbiness of true age.

The 'bum-bra' (left) that raises the buttocks helps to give a more youthful contour. The face-lift ('before': below left; 'after': below right) increases sex appeal by recreating youthful skin-signals. While the elderly wish to appear young, the very young (as in this tiny tots beauty pageant) (right) wish to appear older: everyone wants to be 21.

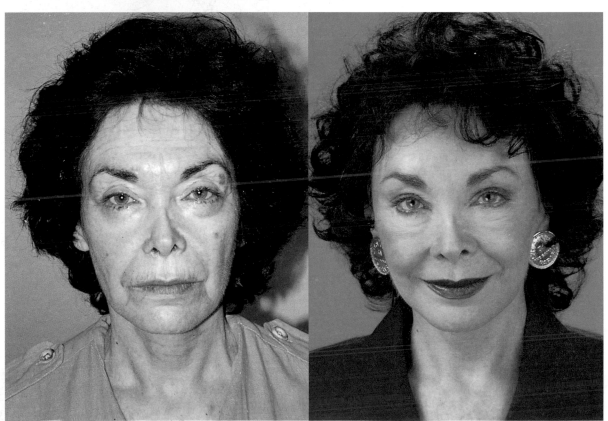

Women are not alone in this. The urge to look young is one of the factors behind the strange male activity of face-shaving. Many adult males the world over waste a considerable amount of time during their lives scraping off their adult male badge, the beard. If they spend roughly 10 minutes a day on this task, that adds up to a total of about 132 days, or 19 weeks, in a 70-year life span.

It has been said that the advantages of this strange procedure are six-fold: (1) it makes the man look younger, because boys do not have beards; (2) it makes him look cleaner, because beards act as a scent-trap and food-trap; (3) clean-shaven faces look more expressive, because beard-removal renders changing facial expressions more visible; (4) they seem more friendly, because the jutting beard exaggerates the aggressively jutting male jaw; (5) they demonstrate greater sensitivity, because he is prepared to take trouble over his appearance; and (6) a clean-shaven man looks more feminine, and is therefore less of a sexual threat to women.

All this is true, but today the most important of these six factors is undoubtedly the one to do with reducing age. The clean-shaven chin gives the male face a boyish look that helps to make its owner seem much younger than he really is.

Shaving began in ancient times as an act of humiliation. Prisoners and slaves were shaved to rob them of their virility. Some devout men shaved themselves voluntarily as a gesture of humility before their gods. Later, in ancient Greece and Rome, soldiers were ordered to shave to distinguish themselves from hairy barbarians in the heat of battle and to protect themselves from being grabbed by the beard in hand-to-hand combat. As these early functions of shaving faded into the past, the custom of beard-removal, having already developed a powerful social momentum, managed to survive in its new role as a youth-enhancing device. As male life spans grew longer and longer under modern conditions, the need to imitate a youthful appearance also increased and shaving developed into a global pursuit.

For an ageing female a different problem exists. Her facial skin, so taut and smooth when she is young, becomes looser and more wrinkled with the passage of time. The solution open to her is far more challenging than a ten-minute shave. For her, the ultimate answer is to opt for cosmetic surgery. By subjecting herself to the surgeon's knife a middle-aged female can regain her youthful appearance by having her facial skin stretched

53

and tightened. Today she can choose between a face-lift, an eyelid-lift, an eye-bag lift, a chemical skin peel or dermabrasion.

The face-lift is a three-hour operation. A surgeon describes it in the following words: 'I begin my incision in the scalp in the temporal area. Then I come down just in front of the ear and I follow the ear around the lobe…and then into the posterior hairline…I then separate the skin from the tissue beneath it…I loosen the skin totally from the temple to the outer end of the eyebrow, over the cheeks, and halfway down the neck. I raise the skin-flap and expose the tissue underneath…Next I draw the skin back and up, trim off the excess, and suture the skin into its new place.' This is clearly not a procedure for the faint-hearted, and its growing popularity reveals just how much value is placed on signals of youthfulness by the modern female.

A strange side-effect of the desire to look like the youngest of adults is the invention of the 'Tiny Tots Beauty Pageant'. While the middle-aged want to look like teenagers again, the youngest of children, those who have not yet reached puberty, want to look older. Today everyone, it seems, wants to look 21 – the sexiest age available to the human animal.

Another key signal of youthfulness is the waist/hip ratio of the female. When she is a child there is little difference between the two measurements, and when she is much older there will again be only a small difference. The age for maximum difference – very small waist contrasting with wide hips – is again that magical period in the early 20s. The ideal ratio for women is 0.7 (waist to hip), compared with 0.9 for males. This has universal appeal, a fact which can be tested by a simple experiment. If a set of life-size, cut-out female silhouettes is constructed and placed in a row in a public place, such as a shopping mall, it is possible to ask passers-by to register which particular waist/hip ratio they find most appealing. When this test was carried out in the shopping centre of an English city where there were many tourists as well as local people, it was possible to ensure that those responding to the shapes had come from a wide variety of cultural backgrounds. Despite this, there was a general consensus and one particular silhouette was preferred by almost everyone. Needless to say, it was the magical 0.7 ratio.

This result is not so surprising when the findings from another investigation are considered. It was discovered that women with a smaller contrast between waist and hips were less likely to conceive when they attended a fertility clinic. The odds of conceiving declined by 30 per cent with a decrease of only 10 per cent of the waist/hip contrast. In other words, a women with a 0.9 ratio was a third less likely to conceive than one with a 0.8 ratio. Bearing this in mind, it is easier to understand why men unconsciously react more strongly to an hourglass shape than to a straight-bodied woman. And it is easier to understand why, at the age when she is ideally equipped to start breeding, the human female displays this waist/hip contrast most strongly.

Signs of Health

Healthiness is the other universal feature of human sex appeal. In all cultures of the world signs of disease or poor health transmit a strong negative appeal. Skin blemishes are universally disliked, with the result that for centuries there has been a massive cosmetic industry dispensing dermal cover-ups of one kind or another. From ancient Egypt to modern America faces have been powdered, creamed, caked and painted to produce the perfect complexion.

The sophisticated complexity of cosmetics in the ancient world is astonishing. The early Egyptians, for example, used purple, blue and green eye-shadow, the green eye-paint being made from malachite, which they ground on beautiful stone palettes. They defined their eyebrows with black antimony powder; exaggerated their eyelids with galena made from lead ore; etched their eyes with a mixture of ground-up ants' eggs; painted their faces with ceruse; added ochre to colour their cheeks and carmine to redden their lips. They also used coan quince cream to smooth their complexions; applied cleansing oils made from wild castor plants; employed hydrosilicate of copper to counteract sunburn; smoothed away their wrinkles with masks of egg white; and concocted antiseptic perfumes from markorum, saffron, rose-water, panther, chypre, balm, honey, crocus, lotus, vine, aromatic herbs, burnt resin and scented woods.

The cosmetic traditions of the ancient Middle East travelled around the globe, being simplified, modified and varied, but rarely improved upon. Indeed, there were times when the heavy make-up of Europeans became a serious health hazard. Instead of covering up signs of ill-health, they caused it.

Today, science has stepped in to render all modern cosmetics safe to the skin, and the industry has reached new heights of which even the ancient pharaohs would be proud. It

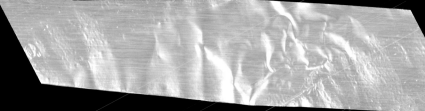

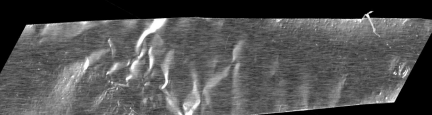

has been calculated that in a single year recently Europeans alone spent no less than £15.5 billion ($25 billion) on cosmetics and toiletries. Even corpses in their coffins are now given cosmetic attention to make them look 'healthier' before being placed on view in funeral parlours, a development of their ancient craft which the early Egyptians would undoubtedly have approved.

But displays of health are not only a question of looks, they are also a matter of movement. Anyone who demonstrates robust energy and maximum vigour will automatically transmit sexual signals to onlookers. This is the essence of that uniquely American innovation, the cheerleader display. Cheerleaders transmit strong sex appeal to young men, not because they perform wickedly sexy dancing, or because they demonstrate intensely competitive athletic skill, but because they exhibit movements that emanate boundless good health. Their routines are carefully designed to display this without straying into the slinky actions of the bar-dancer, or the muscle-straining exertions of the serious athlete. The movements of the cheerleaders somehow manage to occupy a centre ground between these two extremes and, in so doing, focus our attention on their body flexibility and their well-balanced, curvaceous strength. These girls, by their training and their lifestyles, are the very epitome of good health and, through it, of glowing sex appeal.

Demonstrations of health are of value to any young adults wishing to advertise themselves as potential sexual partners. To this end, all over the world, in almost every culture, they can be found performing strange, rhythmic movements in front of one another. They want to indicate their physical fitness but without engaging in anything as competitive as sport or gymnastics. So they gyrate in front of one another, enacting symbolic locomotion that goes nowhere. We call it dancing. The energetic actions of the dancers suggest vigorous physical qualities that translate well into strong procreative potential.

A characteristic of the young adult female is that her breasts do not yet sag. This special quality is emphasized by the notorious American 'wet T-shirt' competition.

If the roots of dancing are traced back it emerges that there were two specific contexts in which it originally took place: when people were working themselves up to attack or to mate. The war dance and the erotic dance were both important to early societies, but today only the latter has any significance. War dancing has been largely reduced to the level of a commercial presentation by corrupted tribespeople for adventurous tourists. Everywhere else the underlying message of the modern dance is purely sexual. It has become a major part of the cultural exaggeration of human gender signals at social gatherings all around the globe, from small private parties to huge public carnivals, from glitteringly bright dance halls to dimly lit discos, and from elegant night-clubs to sleazy nude cabarets.

Phallic Symbolism

Although intense, the sexual language of dancing is usually implicit rather than explicit. Overt genital displays are extremely rare. The display themes are usually derived from the earlier stages of the human courtship sequence. The later stages are represented by a certain amount of sinuous writhing and thrusting, but there is usually a degree of abstraction that makes them fall short of copulatory mimicry. For erotic displays based on the extremes of sexual arousal we must look elsewhere, to the realms of phallic symbolism.

The contrasting shape of the external genitals is one of the most basic of all human gender signals. For many animals the external genitals appear the same in the two sexes – simply a male aperture and a female aperture which are pressed together when mating takes place. But for humans and other mammals the male has a protruding penis that becomes enlarged during sexual arousal. This act of enlargement has become a worldwide symbol of male virility and has come to play a central role in erotic mythology.

For some men the desire to display a large phallus is so strong that they resort to extreme measures. In the Philippines there is a popular form of erotic surgery in which small plastic balls called *bulitas* are used to enlarge the penises of young Filipino males who wish to give added sexual pleasure to their partners. The plastic pellets (bought from fairground shooting galleries) are inserted beneath the skin of the penis where they create hard, protruding lumps that provide increased stimulation to the female genitals. They also, in all probability, add considerably to the sexual status of the males concerned, indicating just how far they are prepared to go to improve their sex lives.

Some men, distraught at what they perceive as inferior penis size, have gone even further. A Californian doctor has recently made a fortune from a dramatic penis enlargement operation. It is a kind of liposuction in reverse, with fat taken from elsewhere on the patient's body and injected into his supposedly inadequate sex organ. This increases the girth of the penis, while its length is improved by modifying the base of the organ to release two inches normally held inside the body.

The operation, which takes 40 minutes under general anaesthetic, costs $5,900 (about £4,000) and the good doctor manages about six of these procedures a day. With a sufficient supply of anxious males, this amounts to somewhere in the region of nine million dollars a year. And there appears to be no shortage of customers. At present the doctor is said to be receiving more than 2000 calls a day and has a five-month waiting list. By the end of 1995 he claimed to have enlarged no fewer than 3500 penises. The cult of phallomania even has its own journal, *Penis Power Monthly.*

Clearly men are prepared to pay a high price to stand tall, in the phallic sense. One male model who underwent the ordeal commented afterwards, 'I was average, around 6 inches…now I've got 9 inches, and that's a power buzz – no need for a flash car'.

Another young husband who was treated claimed that his penis width had increased by 40 per cent and that, as a result, his sex life had been considerably 'enlivened'.

There is another and even more bizarre way of creating the impression of increased penis size. This is an indirect approach in which the female makes the male phallus *feel* larger by making her sexual passage narrower. Californian plastic surgeons now routinely perform a fat-grafting operation called 'female genitalia enhancement' for the woman who 'wants to feel tighter'. Fat is taken from the patient's thighs, emulsified and injected into her outer labia. The labia are then squeezed to re-position the fatty tissue in the lateral walls of her vagina. This narrowing of the female tube means that even a small penis will feel huge, both to the male and to his surgically improved partner. And a large penis will feel almost unbearably huge.

This idea of making the penis seem larger by making the female passage smaller is not new. As long ago as the seventeenth century a French professor of surgery was recommending that women could cure vaginal 'looseness' by bathing their genitals in distilled myrtle berry juice, perfumed with clove and ambergris.

Of course, when the confines of the human body are left behind and we move into the realms of sculptural symbolism, then the sky's the limit. Gigantic phallic statues are known from many parts of the world and have been crafted by artists for thousands of years.

It has been argued that prehistoric peoples did not understand the connection between

Penis-size has always been an important male display, as in the massive chalk-cut figure of the 2000 year-old Cerne Abbas Giant in Southern England.

male erection and ejaculation, on the one hand, and pregnancy on the other. Females were clearly involved in reproduction because they produced babies, but the male's role in breeding was supposed to have been overlooked. This ignorance was thought to explain the predominance of the Mother Goddess in early religions. The mother symbolized fecundity and the fertility of the earth, while the father was of little significance. Then, when his role in procreation was eventually understood, the Mother Goddess faded out and the deity became God the Father. This story is appealing, but it cannot be true because the fertilizing power of the phallus was commemorated in ancient art from the earliest times. The cult of the phallus as the symbol of virility is known from the very beginning of the Neolithic period, about 10,000 years ago.

Indeed, the phallus as the source of human life was considered so important that phallic worship became widespread. The Creator, the Supreme Being, was envisaged in the shape of a phallus because he was thought of as procreating the Universe. Amulets depicting an erect penis were frequently worn to call upon the protection of the Great One, rather as today many people will wear a crucifix.

Phallic statues and images were displayed in civilizations all around the Mediterranean. They are known from ancient Egypt as early as 4500 BC, from early Greece and Rome. On the island of Corsica there remain to this day a number of huge penis-shaped megaliths that were erected, in both senses of the word, 5000 years ago. On the island of Malta, according to a Victorian traveller, there was discovered a sculpture of 'four huge phalli, carved out of the solid granite, but which were subsequently metamorphosed by the virtuous Knights of St John, and served for their arms'. This would explain the curious, chopped-off tips of the famous Maltese Cross.

In India the ancient cult of the phallus – known there as the lingam – has continued without interruption right down to the present time. Giant lingams are still garlanded and decorated by the devout, as are similar lingams in Thailand, where they may be seen adorned with coloured silks, flowers and other offerings.

In Japan there is an annual festival every March at Komaka-shi, near Nagoya, where an enormous wooden carved phallus is carried by priests in procession through the streets. After the festivities are over, the new phallus is carefully laid at the side of the entrance pathway to the shrine, alongside the others from previous years. The festival is a prayer for procreation and virility, and it is said that if a woman visits the shrine and strokes one of the gigantic wooden phalluses she will greatly increase her chances of meeting the perfect male partner.

Over the centuries the phallic display of the male became modified and stylized in many ingenious ways. The biologically erect penis became the culturally stiff artefact. It was worn as a protruding codpiece; it was waved by conjurors as a magic wand to make things appear (like babies) from nowhere; it was proudly carried in procession as a royal sceptre; it was brandished as a fool's staff, complete with symbolic testicles in the form of inflated bladders; it was ridden in the sky by witches on the way to their sabbat, when it was euphemistically referred to as a broom handle; it became the towering maypole around which dancers celebrated the rites of spring; and it became the extended finger or forearm of countless obscene gestures.

The last great phallic display in Britain was made about 2000 years ago at Cerne Abbas in Dorset. There, on a conspicuous hillside, a colossal chalk-cut figure nearly 55 m (180 ft) tall of a giant was made, with a spectacularly erect penis rising up in the centre of the body. The penis itself was 9 m (30 ft) long. At one point in its history, the huge organ was carefully obliterated by pious Christians, who viewed it as a pagan horror, but it has since been restored to its former glory. In December 1996, a self-styled pagan priest called for a fertility ritual to be performed on the surface of the penis at the winter solstice. He encouraged childless couples to visit the site and to make love lying on the phallus, in the hope of conjuring up longed-for pregnancies.

Once again, the authority of the phallus was being called upon as the most intense of all male signals, the most potent statement in the language of the sexes. Its enduring power is reflected in the fact that the erect penis is still completely forbidden on any public cinema or television screen. It is permitted to show a gun, which shoots death, but not a penis, which shoots life. By this distinction the twentieth century will be remembered.

Status Displays

A less direct way of performing a sexual display is to demonstrate high status. This can ignore all the usual

In Japan, penis-shrines are places of worship where visitors reverently touch the carved wooden phalluses and pray for fertility (next page).

bodily features. Indeed, a high-status display can make even a physically unappealing individual seem highly desirable. By presenting signs of great wealth or influence, the male or female concerned can transmit signals of sexuality that are based, not on appearance, but on the promise of protective power. The important people who demonstrate their high status by living in magnificent mansions may be old and wrinkled, or perhaps old and de-wrinkled, but they can still exude a strong sex appeal simply by their visible wealth.

For those without possessions, some other display of high status has to be found. Among the nomads of North Africa, for example, the Tuareg tribespeople use an unusual method. Top males in the tribes show their elevated position by the degree to which they hide their faces and silence their tongues. A top male's face is never seen; his expressions are invisible. And his voice is seldom heard. He is an enigma and it is this that gives him his appeal. Only weaker males need to use their voices and their facial expressions to impose themselves on the companions. Top males scorn such weakness.

A different form of status display can be observed wherever one culture is dominant over another. The weaker culture starts to imitate the stronger one. In the days of ancient Egypt, for instance, the nearby tribes were always trying to emulate their affluent neighbours. Both Jewish and Arab tribes tried to copy the Egyptians in certain ways. For instance, they saw that the Egyptians circumcised their young males, so they followed suit. Keeping up with the Egyptians later gave way to keeping up with the Greeks or the Romans. Today it is a case of keeping up with the Americans, or with Europe. Young adults from non-Western cultures can often be found enhancing their status, not by honouring their great and ancient local traditions but by copying certain Western qualities. It is not enough simply to abandon exquisite eastern dress for monotonous, grey Western styles. Facial features must also be changed.

In India there is a thriving business in face-bleaching. There, a whitened face is considered to have high status, making its owner look more Western and, at the same time, indicating that they have not been forced to work in the sun.

Until recently, there was a thriving business in hair-straightening. It is possible to eliminate the crinkles in human hairs simply by ironing them, as one would with crumpled clothing. Black entertainers used to have their fuzzy hair flattened to look more European.

Following the 'black is beautiful' campaign of the 1970s, this largely vanished and entertainers reverted rapidly and proudly to their natural 'Afro' hairstyle.

In Singapore, women flock to have their eyes altered to look more Western. Scorning their attractive Oriental eyefolds – the little epicanthic folds of skin that evolved as a way of protecting their ancestors from the biting cold of the north, where they originated – they welcome the surgeon's knife that skilfully removes them and renders their eyes more occidental in shape.

The same is true in Japan. At one plastic surgery hospital the records of operations performed in a recent year show that no less than 43 per cent were on the eyes, with only 22 per cent on the nose, 12 per cent on the lips, 12 per cent on skin wrinkles, nine per cent on liposuction and two per cent on other features. In a Western country such a clinic would cater largely for women wanting to look younger, but in Japan there is far more emphasis on wanting to look Western. Confirming this is the fact that at the Japanese hospital in question, 49 per cent of the patients were very young, either in their teens or their 20s.

These Japanese operations are motivated primarily by the need for improving social standing through sex appeal. The young women are undergoing surgery to make themselves more attractive to men and therefore more acceptable to prospective employers. In fact, many of the young women visiting the hospital took with them photographs of high-status females, such as supermodels and Hollywood actresses, whom they wished to resemble, in the hope that they too would then gain high status through their looks.

It is curious to think of people from an ancient civilization with a long aesthetic tradition based on its own unique values flocking to surgeons to mimic an alien culture. It is hard to conjure up a convincing picture of, say, a young American woman arriving at a clinic clutching a photograph of an Oriental beauty and asking to have exquisite eyefolds like hers added to an attractive Western face. Yet young Oriental women by the thousand want to look Western. It is a strangely racist statement – a statement against one's own race – to seek to remove the features that typify one's own people. But if it raises status, and therefore sex appeal, there will always be those who are ready to submit themselves to the knife.

Symbols of Courage

In many tribal cultures another way of saying 'I will make a good sexual partner' has been to demonstrate some kind of courage. In the islands of the South Pacific, for example, a tattooed skin has always been considered to be especially attractive. Part of its appeal is that it is so painful to apply that it requires an act of bravery on the part of the person concerned.

The underlying message is that, if you are brave enough to volunteer to subject yourself to the pain of body mutilation merely for the sake of appearances, then you are more likely to be courageous in the defence of your partner or your family, should the need arise. In a similar way, for a woman, undergoing painful body decoration suggests that she will be better able to cope with the pain of childbirth.

Despite this underlying appeal, tattooed skin does not meet with universal approval. People are sharply divided over whether it increases sexual attractiveness or reduces it. Those who take a negative view are probably reacting to the way in which it interferes with that other basic response that finds sexual appeal in a smooth, clear, unblemished skin. For this reason it has remained a minority display, although its occurrence is amazingly widespread.

Tattooing probably began in the Old Stone Age and spread from Europe around the world. Its official functions were to protect the individual from evil spirits, to identify people as belonging to a particular group or faith or to placate the spirits in the afterlife. For some individuals, it was a way of sending a specific message. Some early travellers, for example, would have their last will and testament engraved on their skin to ensure that their final wishes could not be ignored. And in ancient wars messengers were sometimes tattooed with important information on the tops of their shaven heads. When their hair had regrown sufficiently to hide the wording, they were then sent off through enemy lines to deliver the secret messages by means of another close shave.

The Naga of Assam employed tattoos so that husbands and wives could recognize one another in the afterlife. Ainu women tattooed themselves in order to look like their goddess, Aioina. One of the reasons that Native Americans used tattoos was because they believed that, after death, they would be examined for them by guardian spirits and would only be allowed to pass if they displayed the appropriate patterns. Other groups displaying

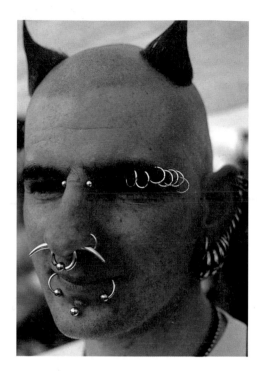

Body-piercing (above) and skin tattooing (right) are visual displays that advertise the ability to withstand pain and therefore, by implication, the ability to show courage in defending a family or (for a woman) when experiencing childbirth.

unusually fine tattoos include the Japanese Yakusa, the Burmese, the Maori of New Zealand, the Samoans and the Marquesans.

The Christian Church took the view that all forms of body decoration were insults to God, who had designed mankind the way he wanted them. John Bulwer, writing on the subject in 1654, entitled his chapter on tattooing, 'Cruell and fantasticall Inventions of Men practised upon their Bodies in a supposed way of Bravery, and wicked practices both of Men and Devils to alter and deforme the Humane Fabricke'. He then went on to describe in great detail all the many tribal examples of the way 'both men and women paint and embroider their skins with iron pens, putting indelible tincture there into...thinking themselves thereby as fine as fivepence in a shower of raine...devillish fine! For, whatsoever is done by abuse of Nature is diabolicall; for, as the right use of the naturall endowments of the body is from God, so the abuse of them is from the Devill.'

As the Christian missionaries spread out across the globe they did their best to suppress all forms of native tattooing, while at the same time being forced to admit that those who subjected themselves to it were 'cruell brave'. This Christian opposition resulted in tattooing becoming an exotic rarity in Europe and it was not until the nineteenth century that a few exhibitionist males had themselves 'decorated like savages'. These men, who always claimed that they had been forced to subject themselves to tattooing while exploring foreign parts, became great fairground attractions and were able to make a good living simply by showing their bodies to paying audiences. The more painful the application of the tattoos had been, the more the crowds marvelled. Some men went to the lengths of having the sensitive palms of their hands covered in fine designs; others went to the extremes of having their eyelids tattooed and even the insides of the mouth and nose. One famous exhibitor, Captain Constantine, who claimed to have been forcibly tattooed by Chinese Tartars in Burma, had every portion of his body decorated with the single exception of the soles of his feet. In all, he had 388 separate motifs on his skin.

In the early part of the twentieth century, tattooing made a massive recovery from Christian suppression, especially among those whose travels took them to parts of the world where local cultures still practised the art. As a result, sailors became strongly associated with tattooing and, at one time, it was estimated that 90 per cent of all naval personnel bore some kind of tattoo. By mid-century the fashion had even spread to famous figures such as Don Juan of Spain, King Frederick of Denmark and Field-Marshal Montgomery of Alamein.

In more recent years, tattooing has become fashionable as a sexual display among the extrovert young, along with various forms of painfully applied, decorative body-piercing such as nose-rings, tongue-studs, nipple-rings and genital ornaments. The drawback with these mutilation displays is that, although they score points as undeniable proof of physical courage, they then inevitably inhibit the vigorous sexual intimacies they have encouraged. As a result they have remained very much an eccentric, minority fashion.

Another flawed form of bravery display is the one employed by all those men who, by choosing a dangerous occupation, attract women who find their risk-taking sexually appealing. The catch here is that the bravery they show in undertaking their hazardous tasks also means that they may be killed carrying them out. The sexual appeal of such life-threatening activities as motor racing or professional boxing acts like a magnet for women who, once emotionally attached to their heroes, then spend their time trying to persuade them to give up the very pursuit that made them glamorous in the first place.

Despite the flaws in these various activities, it has to be said that cowardice has never been sexy. The wimp, the weed, the man who is 'yellow' or 'chicken', the woman who is a fretter, a fusser, an anxious bag of nerves, will always lack sex appeal when compared with more relaxed, adventurous individuals. The fact that the cowards and the fussers may, in the long run, prove to be safer partners does not save them because it is during moments of drama, at times of sudden emergency, that the human partner is put to the most severe test, and it is then that the bold will flourish and come to the rescue.

Signs of Availability

In modern society, gender signalling has become quite complicated. It is not enough merely to send out signals that indicate the arrival of adulthood. In addition, there is a whole complex system of signs indicating beauty, youth, health, virility, status and courage. And there is something else. In many cultures there are specific signals of availability. In other words, a young adult may be displaying all the necessary signs of active sexuality, but is she or he *available* for mating?

In a small tribe this would not be a problem, because everybody would know everybody else and would be able to see clearly what was happening. But supposing a society was more secretive? Supposing, to keep them safe, young girls were shut away and unable to display their feminine appeal? What then? The answer was to provide some kind of formal signal that told the community 'Now she is available'.

Signals of unavailability and availability.
The Maltese 'faldetta' (above) is a sombre
garment that obliterates the female shape
and cries out 'keep away' to any male.
In Tahiti, by contrast, wearing a flower
over the right ear says 'come here, I am
unattached' (right).

A remarkable example of an availability signal is to be found on the Mediterranean island of Malta. In the small villages there, there is a curious architectural feature on many of the older houses. It takes the form of a stone bracket, high up by a first-floor window. Although obsolete for many years, in earlier times this bracket had an important role to play in local gender signalling. If, inside the house, there was a virgin ready for marriage, this bracket was decorated in a special way by placing a pot of basil in it. Basil was the symbolic plant of lovers and its display was a sign to passers-by that a virgin in the house was ready for marriage.

It is reasonable to ask why this basil display was necessary. The answer will seem extraordinary in today's social climate. It was because, in earlier centuries, a young woman was seldom allowed to venture outside her house. It was said, perhaps with slight exaggeration, that she would only appear in public twice in her life: once to be married and once to be buried. Apart from those special occasions she was a recluse, living out her life behind high walls that protected her from all the dangers of the outside world. So, for her, a display of availability of this kind was essential.

Even when rules were relaxed a little and she was allowed outside to go to church, she was required to conceal herself behind Malta's version of the veil, the all-covering *faldetta*. It not only concealed her appearance but also managed to disguise her human shape. It was a forbidding garment that positively shouted 'keep away' to any passing male.

In less restrictive cultures there have been a number of simple clothing signals to indicate availability or non-availability. This has been true in rural Spain and can still be seen today in the fields of Lanzarote in the Canary Islands. There it is possible to distinguish at a glance – and even at a great distance – the unmarried from the married females as they work in the countryside. The unmarried girls wear distinctive white cotton bonnets, while the married women cover their heads with pale brown palm hats. So rigid is this system that there is never the slightest risk of making a mistake.

Western women would be insulted if it was suggested that they should adopt some such system of visual signalling. In some countries it is even insulting to address them as Miss or Mrs. Yet there must be many times when an attractive young woman would prefer to transmit signals that she is not available, rather than repeatedly have to rebuff the advances of hopeful males. At present the Lanzarote females have the advantage over her.

Even in the much more free-and-easy lifestyle of the South Pacific, young adults often adopt a sign of availability to signal to others whether approaches should be made or not. There, as in Malta, the signals are floral, but in this case the flower in question is the more colourful hibiscus. If a young man or woman is available as a possible partner, then the hibiscus blossom is tucked behind the right ear. If not, then it is placed behind the left ear. For those who find it hard to remember such conventions, the clue is that the person whose heart is already taken wears the flower *above* the heart – in other words, on the left-hand side. Rumour has it that it is not unknown for a family man to switch his flower temporarily from left to right ear during an exciting evening out. (The nearest equivalent in the Western world would be the removal of a wedding ring.)

Virginity

A special feature of the human female that has always been of great significance in the language of the sexes is her virginity. It is not something she can display publicly as she goes about her daily life, but its presence or absence has always been of particular interest to men. There is a powerful underlying reason for this.

One primeval sexual inequality that has always existed between men and women is certainty of parentage. A woman always knows that her baby is hers, but for a man there must always be an element of doubt. Is he really the father? For many men this question is laughable. It never crosses their minds that their wives could be unfaithful. To suggest the possibility of such a thing would be grossly insulting to them. And yet, viewed objectively, there is no way they can be absolutely sure of her fidelity unless they have spent every hour of every day in her company. This is almost impossible and, as a result, some insecure men suffer from a nagging uncertainty, a deep-seated feeling of intense jealousy that starts to haunt them day after day.

So obsessed do some men become with the fear of spousal infidelity that many famous legends and droll tales have sprung up around this theme. The most outlandish concerns the husband who, after trying in a thousand ways to catch out his wife, finally decides on the only absolutely foolproof method. He secretly castrates himself so that, when she later bears him a child, he will be able to confront her with her undeniable adultery.

Over the centuries there have been many factual attempts to reduce a husband's uncertainty. Samoan men, for example, when they were about to set off on a journey, were reputed to apply a special yellow paint to the bellies of their wives. If the wives were unfaithful, this would be rubbed off by the friction of their illicit partners and the husbands would detect this on their return. (And any lonely wife collecting a new supply of yellow pigment would obviously become highly suspect.)

There were eye-witness reports that, several centuries ago, the people living to the east of the Black Sea employed a broad girdle on untanned leather to prevent their pubertal girls from becoming sexually active before their wedding night. Girls as young as 10 or 12 were fitted out with these leather girdles which were then stitched tightly into place. (It is not clear how these garments permitted other biological functions.) Then, on their wedding nights, their bridegrooms would ritually cut through the leather with a sharp dagger.

Other methods of ensuring chastity were more brutal. Early travellers returned to Europe with exotic stories of women in far-off lands who were forced to wear a metal fibula, buckle or ring through holes punched in their outer labia, to block any penetration.

It is thought that, when these travellers returned home, the amazing stories they told inspired the European invention of the metal chastity belt, an item of 'clothing' that would not involve mutilation and which was therefore more 'civilized' than genital rings. According to popular legend this infamous device was invented to keep medieval wives faithful while their husbands were away on the Crusades, and to protect their virginal daughters against rape when the men were not there to defend and protect them. The truth is more likely to have been that a metal belt, locked around the female crotch in such a way that copulation was impossible, was first employed in Europe, not by noble knights but by a few eccentric sadists. A fourteenth-century tyrant from Padua called Novello da Carrara took great pleasure in inflicting ingenious tortures on his prisoners and, among his cruel instruments dating from the end of that century was an iron collar and a 'girdle of chastity' which he is said to have forced his mistresses to wear.

The earliest published record of a chastity belt dates from 1405. The drawing shows a clumsy instrument said to have been in use in Florence. Metal girdles for women were reported to have been on sale in a St Germain market in Paris in the sixteenth century. A little later, in the seventeenth century, an engraving entitled 'The jealous husband prepares for a journey' shows a naked wife wearing a chastity belt and trying to take the key from

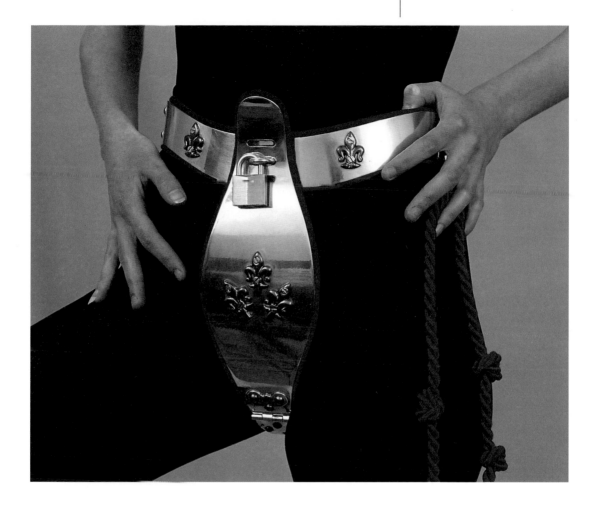

The modern chastity belt, beautifully crafted in velvet-lined brass, is more likely to be used for sexual titillation than for its original function of sexual control.

her departing husband's hand. Various examples of antique chastity belts are also known from a number of European museums, but the truth is that there is no evidence that this device was ever seriously used on a wide scale. It seems to have been a sexual curiosity reserved largely for romantic fictions and the occasional obsessive libertine.

Today these belts are still being made and worn, although they are now employed more for sexual titillation than for sexual control. They play a part in bondage rituals and are worn by those individuals who find unusual forms of 'dressing up' sexually exciting. These new models are works of art – made to measure and carefully crafted so that they do not cause any discomfort. Individually fashioned in brass, velvet-lined, with lockable padlocks and costing as much as $600, they have become objects of erotic *haute couture*. It is true that they effectively prevent penetration, and it is rumoured that certain elderly males have recently employed them in earnest to curb their young wives' sexual generosity, but despite male fantasizing they remain a rarity and no more than an oddity in the history of European gender relations.

One exceptional example of the use of a modern chastity belt, however, concerns a rape victim who was so traumatized by her experience that she was unable to enjoy a normal sex life with her husband. She lived in constant fear of being raped a second time, and this fear made her frigid. To save their marriage she took to wearing a specially designed chastity belt that enabled her to go anywhere without being haunted by her obsessive anxiety. Gradually she was able to relax and, as the years passed, her normal sex life with her husband was resumed. So, in this special case at least, there may be a serious role for the much ridiculed, protective chastity belt.

In some tribal societies where virginity is prized, the ceremonies to ensure it are comparatively mild and harmless, causing little more than social embarrassment. For example, young girls of the Irabo tribe in Nigeria undergo a public coming-of-age breast inspection. Watched by an enthusiastic audience, they must submit themselves to a naked breast check by older women to ensure that they have not given milk and are therefore (supposedly) still virgins. They submit to this ordeal reluctantly and then, in a quaint moment of bureaucratic formality, have their condition officially rubber-stamped, so that they can collect their certificates of virginity.

In many countries a wedding ritual is introduced to prove that the bride was a virgin when she married. In some regions, such as North Africa and parts of the Middle East, a bloody bedsheet is hung from the window of the bridal chamber, demonstrating that the bride bled when her hymen was ruptured by her new husband. On others, her bloody bloomers are paraded through the streets for all the wedding guests to see. Fortunately for some brides, there is usually a hapless domestic animal available to provide some blood if a little extra help is needed with this particular ritual. (In certain instances it is known that brides who have already lost their virginity have been provided – usually by their anxious mothers – with small bladders containing fresh animal blood. These are secreted under a pillow and can be burst with a sharp fingernail at the crucial moment.)

One way to reduce the risk of a young wife being unfaithful is to reduce her sexual pleasure. This can be done by surgically removing her external genitals. Brutally shorn of her clitoris and labia, she will experience virtually no erotic arousal and secret sex will have little meaning for her. In this mutilated condition she will lack any motivation for indulging in sexual adventures, either before she is married, or, for that matter, afterwards.

This savage operation, generally known as female circumcision, is a hallowed social custom in several parts of the world. Sadly, this is not a tribal rarity. It is happening today on a massive scale in Africa and the Middle East. It robs young girls of their biological birthright, and, what is worse, it is not performed by brutal men but by older women. In some regions girls are not only mutilated in this way, but are also stitched up afterwards so that, even if a rogue male manages to get to them, he will not be able to penetrate them. Their virginity will be safe until, on their wedding night, they are ceremonially unstitched by their husbands (see Chapter 6).

All over the world, different cultures have imposed their local dialects on the language of the sexes. Some have tried to suppress it, restrain it and control it. Others have joyously exaggerated and amplified it. But, one way or another, boy has had to meet girl, make love and produce children. Out of sexual arousal some kind of family life has to grow. What form this takes is the subject of the next chapter.

3

Patterns of Love

In the centre of old Amsterdam there are some unusual window displays. Some of the narrow streets that run alongside the famous canals are lit up at night with splashes of red. Each red patch, on closer inspection, is a small shop window in which sits a scantily clad young woman. As with all shop windows, the contents on display are for sale, for this is Amsterdam's notorious red light district where, for a small fee, these women will copulate briefly with any man who is prepared to pay for the service. There are several thousand of these window-girls and, despite all the recent anxieties about the risk of contracting Aids, business is still booming, as it is in the brothel districts of almost every major city in the world.

Consider what happens inside one of these red-light cubicles. This is human sexuality reduced to its bare minimum. It is more like a quick visit to a dentist to relieve a pain than a romantic interlude. The man is washed, excited, inserted, climaxed and dispatched. It is a brief, efficient extraction, leaving the patient feeling better, but strangely ill-at-ease. Even the most dedicated visitor to these haunts must know that what is being performed is a mere remnant of human sexual life. This unconscious knowledge creates within him, not gratitude for the service performed, but an odd kind of resentment, an unspoken hostility that sees the girls concerned treated, not as doctors or nurses curing an unfortunate condition, but relegated to the fringes of society as somehow unwholesome.

Why should human sexual behaviour express itself in this way? Why is the strange phenomenon of prostitution such a global industry? Human beings feel happy and secure inside a loving family unit, so what is happening here? How can the sexual encounters offered by these girls have any meaning for a species that forms lasting pair-bonds?

Part of the answer has to do with the size of modern-day communities. Prostitution and many of the other unusual human mating arrangements were only possible when the primeval villages in which our species evolved, over a

The window-girls of Amsterdam's famous red light district offer the most abbreviated form of human sexual involvement.

million years, grew into bustling towns. There, in unnaturally crowded conditions, all kinds of sexual experiments were able to flourish. Each adult was faced with a huge variety of possible partners and the human urge to seek novelty did the rest.

In primeval times it had not been like that. Back in the prehistoric past, when tribes were compact, technology was primitive and our human numbers were few, the choice of a partner was severely limited. As the voices of the boys deepened and the breasts of the girls became swollen, the changing hormones of the young adults spurred them on to find a mate. And they did not have far to look. Nor did they have many qualities to weigh up. If a member of the opposite sex displayed the biological gender signals – male beard and wide male shoulders, or female breasts and wide female hips – then there was little more to consider.

We can only guess at precisely how this primeval scene was played out, but a clue comes from those tribes that still, today, live in small groups in the comparative affluence of the tropical forests. The Baka pygmies from West Africa, for instance, retain many of the characters – indeed many of the advantages – of our remote ancestors. When they pair off at puberty they encounter few of the restrictions or controls that modern urban teenagers must face. All that is needed is some form of incest avoidance, and beyond that there are few obstacles to overcome. We often talk of 'tribal taboos', but the truth is that there are far more 'urban taboos'. Boy-meets-girl in the forest is a joyfully straightforward business. Boy-meets-girl in the city is another matter altogether.

Meeting the Opposite Sex

All over the world the simple business of meeting the opposite sex has become a special challenge, if only because of the sheer size of the human communities. How *do* you start to search for a suitable mate?

In many countries around the shores of the Mediterranean there is an old tradition that helps. It sees young people gathering together each evening as the sun sets and the relentless heat of the day recedes. They stroll up and down in a misleadingly aimless way, taking the evening air and at the same time carefully weighing up the possibilities that the opposite sex has to offer.

Many of these young adults are in one-sex groups, still clinging to their earlier, childhood gangs, which will soon fragment under the growing pressure of sexual interest. As contacts are made across the divide that separates these groups, couples split away and adopt that unmistakable mood of exclusivity so characteristic of young lovers-to-be. Pair-bonds begin to form and new attachments start to gain momentum. For these fortunate young people, modern society has failed to complicate the process of pairing to any great degree and they are able to move smoothly from childhood groups to adult couples without any serious interference.

In the bigger cities today young adults are more likely to need some kind of assistance. Professional organizers step in and the casual parade becomes a specially structured event, an event at which there will only be socially appropriate members of the opposite sex present. It is as if, from within the city super-tribe, a smaller tribe is cocooning itself against outsiders. Social class is supposed to be a thing of the past in our modern, egalitarian world, but when it comes to the serious business of finding a mate, the old class prejudices resurface and vigorously reassert their unwritten rules of 'belonging' or 'not belonging'. In romantic fiction up-town girls may fall in love with down-town boys, and vice versa, but in reality such matings are rare and seldom successful.

Specially arranged events where boy and girl can meet are more common at the upper levels of the social scale. At exclusive dances and balls organized for the young of the rich, the participants can let themselves go in the safe knowledge that everyone else attending the event is from the same background. There will be no embarrassing mistakes, social gaffes or awkward moments. Within the safety of the new tribal net, restraints can be lifted and safe risks can be taken.

The ever-expanding middle class is not so fortunate. There, where young adults are, with undue haste, aimed firmly at long-distance career prospects, the workplace soon comes to dominate their lives. They become so wrapped up in their business careers that they have little time to spare for lengthy forays into the world of pair-bonding or partner-seeking. Some work arenas may provide the necessary supply of potential partners, but others do not. One solution, then, is for modern technology to come to the rescue. Dating agencies, once viewed as a last resort, are becoming increasingly fashionable. Computer dating has lost its stigma and many young adults are now using the short cut that the computer can offer them.

For others, the net is cast even wider. Instead of a national search for a mate, the quest becomes global. The net becomes the internet. Aircraft full of American males in search of loving brides land regularly at Moscow airport. The men in question have made the long journey because on the computer screens back home they have been able to punch up pictures and personal details of extremely beautiful and highly qualified Russian women.

These pairing tours to find perfect Russian mates are highly respectable, but not always successful, due to the widely differing backgrounds of the potential partners. The technology that brings the couples together may be able to match common interests and levels of intelligence and education but it cannot help where different local customs and traditions are concerned. Despite this, the hopeful American males keep arriving, regardless of the fact that there is a large surplus of adult females back home in the United States. They come to Russia with love, and with the documents to prove it.

Once there, the men gather in the hall of a large hotel to meet and interview their prospective brides. The young women are all attractive and eager to settle down and start a family in the West, where they see a better economic future for themselves than in the post-communist chaos of modern Russia. All that is needed is a spark of chemistry between particular males and particular females. The women move from man to man, talk, discuss, get to know one another and then move on again. At the end of this mass mating ritual, some will attempt to take the process further. Others will sadly find no-one with whom they feel suited. To a primitive tribesperson failure in the face of such variety would be unthinkable, but in the modern world we have become so choosy, we have so many factors to consider, that it is not easy and many will go home disappointed – both the men and the women.

Part of the problem is that we have increasingly developed complex standards of social conduct, personality, sex appeal and beauty. We are not satisfied unless our prospective partner can pass a whole series of unwritten, unspoken tests. As we go through this testing process we are not even aware, ourselves, of precisely what the questions are, or what answers we are seeking, but we know when we get them and we also know, with a sombre sinking feeling, when we do not.

The Pair-Bond

Once boy and girl have met and started a relationship of increasing intimacy, a pair-bond will begin to form between them. This powerful feeling of mutual attachment will grow stronger and stronger until the couple becomes a fully fledged pair. Of course, the process can break down at any stage, if one partner starts to have reservations about the other, but before long, if this does not happen, the couple will become emotionally bonded to one another. This entails two major changes in behaviour.

First, the couple no longer think of what they can get out of each other, but what they can give to each other. All adult human beings are essentially selfish, in the sense that they protect themselves from harm. This means that they will always have reservations about making themselves vulnerable to other adults. They will hold themselves back to some extent in adult relationships, just in case they might be betrayed. The process of falling in love sees this restraint dissolved. Eventually the two members of a loving couple are acting essentially as one 'survival unit'. They are no longer two individuals but one 'being' inhabiting two shared bodies. They give to one another without question.

Second, the couple will start to eliminate others from their intimacy. The pairing sequence is essentially an excluding process. The couple not only become positively attached to one another, they also, at the same time, become detached from others. Intense feelings of jealousy can develop at this stage and may create problems where there is competition for affection. Old friendships suffer as the new bond strengthens. Close friends may feel rejected. Family members may encourage the new pair-bond because it increases the chance of continuing the family line through the procreation of a new generation. But non-family friends may begin to feel ousted from their previously intimate relationships and beneath the words of congratulation there are sometimes disguised elements of hostility.

This pair-bonding behaviour is so powerful and so widespread in our species that it appears to be an inborn feature of the human animal. In other words, we are programmed to fall in love and set up a family breeding unit. Since this is not typical of our closest relatives, the monkeys and apes, how has this come about? The answer lies in our hunting past. The highly efficient division of labour into male hunters and female food-gatherers made two special demands on our species. The males had to leave the females behind at a camp site while they hunted and, once on the hunt, the males had to co-operate with one another if they were to succeed in killing large prey. Such a radical change in lifestyle demanded a new type of sexual system.

If the males were to leave the females behind, without their protection, it became important that the two sexes should have some sort of powerful bonds of attachment, one for another. And if the males were to co-operate actively with one another on the hunt, there could be no tyrants in the group. These demands inevitably favoured one particular kind of sexual system, namely the pair-bond, in which each male had his own female and was not therefore in constant conflict with his male companions. For the females, the pair-bond meant that the males would return to the camp site with the spoils of the hunt and share the feast with them. They in turn would share their gathered foods.

This highly successful social system led to the evolution of a powerful, biologically based pairing urge in the rapidly spreading tribes of primeval humans. Monogamy became the norm. Each adult became programmed to stay with a breeding partner long enough to jointly rear a 'serial litter' of young. Because these young were not all born together, but one at a time over a number of years, the pair-bond had to be more than just seasonal or annual. It had to be long lasting if it was to operate at its most efficient.

Today, the evidence of this ancient inheritance is everywhere. Although there are many variations, the central sexual theme remains the family, with a mated pair and their children forming the basic reproductive unit. When a young couple have gone through the pairing process and have committed themselves to one another, they usually celebrate their new condition by declaring eternal love for one another, swearing that they will remain faithful to one another for the rest of their lives. In many countries, to emphasize this declaration of loyalty, they perform a small ritual. They buy a wedding ring. This familiar action carries a powerful symbolic message because the ring, circling the finger like their declared love, has no end. It is an ancient token of eternity that has been employed since the time of the early Egyptians. The first known finger ring dates from the Old Kingdom in 2800 BC.

The same symbolism can be observed on a more dramatic scale at a strange landmark in Estonia, in Northeastern Europe. A small lake appeared there inside a crater formed when a meteor struck the earth. Because, like a wedding ring, the rim of the lake is circular and has no end, it too has become a symbol of eternity. When they are married, an Estonian bride and groom, accompanied by their wedding guests, walk ceremonially around the crater to ensure that their newly blessed love will last forever.

The Collapse of the Pair-Bond

If one takes a close look at modern marriages it soon becomes clear that all is not well with human monogamy. Despite the declarations of eternal love, a large percentage of couples do not last the course. Marital disputes, separations and divorces are increasingly commonplace.

Why should this be? Living in pairs gives us the enormous advantage of doubling the parental care we can offer our children by offering them protection from two parents instead of one. Bearing in mind the tremendously long period of dependence of our species, this makes a great deal of sense. The human mother needs all the help she can get. But why should there be a need to make such a valuable paired condition legally binding? If we evolved as a loving, pair-bonding species, as it seems we did, then why do we need such elaborate wedding ceremonies? The answer, quite simply, is that the bond of attachment between a male and a female is not as invincible as it might be.

This is no accident. In ancient times it was important that, if a male was killed when hunting or a female died in childbirth, the surviving partner would not be 'reproductively wasted'. If being paired meant that the partners would remain faithful for ever, no matter what, then this could mean that a healthy adult was condemned to a lifetime without any further reproductive activity. Similarly, if one partner turned out to be infertile or impotent, their mate's potential would be lost to the tribe. It followed that, for reproductive efficiency, the bond of attachment between male and female had to be strong enough to be long lasting if all was well, but breakable if things went seriously wrong. This built-in weakness would work well enough in primeval conditions, but under the abnormal pressures of modern urban living it could easily misfire. Under stress, the emotional attachment could be broken even when both partners were still alive and well.

By introducing social controls through wedding rituals, religious controls through sacred marriage ceremonies and legal controls through marriage laws, cultures do their

best to tighten the bonds of attachment from the outside, *The new Quickcourt divorce-*
while biology is busy tightening them from the inside. *dispensing machine. In the US*
Despite this, pair-bonds are collapsing all over the world. *it is now possible to obtain*

In the United States the situation is now so bad that one *divorce papers almost as easily as*
out of every three marriages will eventually fail. Each year, *choosing a record on a juke-box.*
two out of every 100 married American women will seek
divorce. (In Canada and the main European countries it averages out at one per 100.)

So many people are now filing for divorce in America that the legal machinery of the
country is becoming clogged up with all the necessary documentation. A new invention
has been brought into play to solve this problem called the automatic divorce dispenser,
which is a vending machine that draws up divorce papers while you wait. These machines
are placed in convenient venues such as public libraries where, in a small booth, it is

possible to tap in your particulars and, for a small fee (the machine accepts all major credit cards), press a button and receive your divorce documents on the spot. These can then be taken straight to a court, by-passing lawyers or other forms of legal aid, and can be handed over for further processing. It makes divorce cheap, quick and easy. The vending machine is appropriately named the 'Quickcourt' and it is becoming increasingly popular in the various states where it has already been installed.

If pairing is so reproductively valuable to our species, then why has evolution not devised some way of keeping our loving emotions more resistant to boredom? Part of the answer has to do with the primeval breeding rate. Back in the days before contraception was available, the mated pairs will have gone from one pregnancy to the next. Today we not only limit our breeding rate drastically, but we also enjoy a much longer life span. So today's loving couple will enjoy much more unencumbered sex than ever before. And this is not the only factor working against the pair-bond...

The Wandering Eye

Almost every day of his adult life, every healthy male commits adultery. He may only do it with his eyes, but every time he sees an attractive woman walk past he stares at her in an unmistakable way. In his mind he is rapidly contemplating what it would be like to make love to her. If circumstances permit, and they rarely do, he may take this further. He is not interested in setting up a new pair-bond, merely in scattering his genetic material as widely as possible. He may not be around to take care of the extra children that may result from his actions, but a few of these additional offspring may survive, even without his help. They will carry on his genes, and that will be enough to keep this type of behaviour from dying out.

All over the world, the same pattern can be observed as boys try to pick up girls, not to establish long-term family units but simply to have uncomplicated sex with them. The girls, whether married or single, usually resist this because, should they become pregnant, they will be left with a heavy maternal burden as one-parent breeding units. But they do not always resist. The human sex drive is strong. And so the boys never give up hope.

It could be argued that, in reality, young men on the lookout for a quick fling are hardly ever hoping to create a pregnancy. On the contrary, the idea of that happening may horrify them and they may go to great lengths to avoid it. So where is the evolutionary advantage in such behaviour? All it does is to start a sequence that is going nowhere and which may cause havoc if it gets out of hand. The answer is that, in primeval times, before the days of efficient contraceptives, such behaviour may well have led to scattered, additional offspring. This will have been enough to keep the male urge to 'score' as part of the genetic programming. It will ensure that the sight of an attractive young woman is sexually appealing to the human male, regardless of whether he is single or an already fully committed member of a family unit.

Many married men find themselves behaving this way occasionally. Their everyday, inner thoughts escalate into rare outward actions. This may happen while, at the same time, they live out their lives as loving fathers and otherwise responsible husbands. The deception involved often leads to high drama and marital distress, but it is surprising how many marriages manage to survive such disruptions.

The female situation is slightly different. She is more strongly tied to the family unit, but she too is less than totally faithful. When she sees a handsome, physically strong young male, she, like her mate, may commit fleeting mental adultery. The enthusiastic female audiences at male strip shows leave little doubt about this. If her mate is older and a good protector but lacks the virility of the young male, she may well accept the latter's advances and become secretly pregnant by him. In evolutionary terms she then has the best of both worlds. The better protector looks after her children; the more virile male gives her his genetic material. Providing the strategy is not discovered, she can then persuade her mated male to rear the children she has obtained in this way.

This pattern of love is more common than most men realize. It does not mean that the woman concerned is not a loving, caring wife, merely that she is driven on by her genes to produce the best offspring that she can. Of course if her mate is both a good protector and a virile young male, then she has all she needs within her family unit and will remain completely faithful.

Various attempts have been made to strengthen the embattled pair-bond artificially. One of the oldest of these is the anti-boredom strategy. It was argued that, if sex between the mated partners could be made more exciting, they would stand a better chance of remaining faithful to one another. Repeating the sex act in an unvarying manner, time after time after time as the married years passed, creates the risk of boredom. By suggesting sexual novelties to the couple, it was thought that new life could be put back into a relationship. For centuries there have been manuals giving sexual advice as to how this could be done. One of the oldest of these is the *Kama Sutra*.

The Kama Sutra of Vatsyayana was written in India in the third century AD and is remarkable for two things. First, it gives as much importance to the female's active sexual involvement and pleasure as it does to the male's. On the pages of this ancient book she is no modest, shy prude lying still and suffering the sexual abandon of her male lover. The female of the *Kama Sutra* is the sexual equal of her male: 'By union with men the lust, desire or passion of women is satisfied and the pleasure derived from the consciousness of it is called their satisfaction'.

Second, it presents a huge variety of sexual actions and positions. There are different kinds of embrace, which are given special names: the touching embrace, the rubbing embrace, the piercing embrace and the pressing embrace, the twining of a creeper, climbing a tree, mixing of seed and rice, and the milk and water embrace. These are not as innocent as they may sound. The milk and water embrace, for example, occurs, 'When a man and a woman…embrace each other as if they were entering into each other's bodies…while the woman is sitting on the lap of the man'.

There are many kinds of kisses, including the nominal, the throbbing, the touching, the straight, the bent, the turned, the clasped, the pressed and the greatly pressed. There is also marking or scratching with the nails, creating a whole variety of small love scars. To give one example, 'When a curved mark is made on the breasts by means of the five nails, it is called a peacock's tail'. Eight different forms of playfully erotic biting to be performed during love-making are also discussed at length. Again, they are given special names. For instance, 'When biting is done with all the teeth, it is called the "line of jewels".'

There are also four kinds of body strikes and eight sounds that may be emitted when experiencing them. Finally, there are all the many body positions for the lovers to test, including such delights as the yawning position, the clasping position, the low congress, the twining position,

The carvings on ancient Indian temples show the way in which sexual pleasure was once encouraged (next page).

93

the mare's position and the 'fixing of a nail'. The book warns that this last position 'is learnt by practice only'.

It is clear from scanning the pages of this ancient work that, before the repressive prudery of the West was imposed on other cultures by mentally warped priests and emotionally crippled missionaries, uninhibited sexual joy was encouraged in both sexes.

Only when the clammy hands of God's various (but always male) earthbound agents came to rest on a society's sexual pleasures did guilt, sin and shame start to spread like a three-pronged epidemic. This was no accident, of course, because once the damage had been done only God's agents could cure it. In this way, and thanks to their own meddling, they had cleverly acquired a job for life.

Many young couples find that one way to keep their pair-bond strong is to pander to their wildest sexual fantasies, but without turning to new partners. In other words, they are unfaithful to one another *with* one another.

In Japan there are special establishments where this is made easy. Officially called 'Boutique Hotels' but popularly known as 'Love Hotels', they are designed to provide outlandish settings where couples can come for an evening's erotic entertainment in exotic circumstances. The design of the hotels is discreet, anonymity being a top priority. For example, special covers are provided to mask the couple's car numberplates when they arrive in the hotel garage. In the reception area, checking in is done through small, low windows so that there is no face-to-face contact between the visitors and the hotel staff. The elevators from the foyer of the hotel only travel up to the rooms. There are separate exit elevators to the garage area, so that guests arriving never encounter other guests leaving.

Inside the rooms there are unusual facilities, such as vibrating beds, water beds, jacuzzis, pornographic television channels, a variety of sex toys and a video camera set up in such a way that the couple can tape their own activities. The decor of each room is strikingly different. In one it is possible to make love in an imported Venetian gondola floating on water. In another it is possible to make love on the back seat of a Rolls Royce. In yet another it is possible to enjoy the amusements of a fully equipped dungeon. Other themes include Orient Express, Space Lab, Blue Submarine and Pink Cadillac. Couples can try different rooms on different occasions, keeping their erotic fantasies fully occupied and thereby enriching their sex lives. For some this is all too organized and contrived, but for others it works well enough.

Prostitution

One of the most common hazards faced by the adulterous male is the escalation of a brief flirtation into a full-blown affair. Some men find that they can maintain a public wife and a private mistress simultaneously. For others the strain is too great (or their secret is discovered) and they are then faced with making a difficult choice. Whatever they do at this stage there is bound to be agony.

To avoid this, many men have, for centuries, employed the services of a professional, that is, a prostitute. Visiting a 'house of pleasure' is quick and efficient with no risk of forming a new pair-bond that will compete with the existing one. Assuming that safe sex is practised and that there are no health risks, it has been argued that visits of this kind may, in some cases, actually help to keep a long-established pair-bond from collapsing. It can do this in one of two ways. If a husband is enjoying a successful and happy marriage in all non-sexual ways with a wife who is a good companion socially, intellectually and parentally, but who is failing to satisfy his sexual needs, he can fulfil those by visiting a prostitute. If this prevents him from abandoning the marriage altogether then it can be said to serve a useful function.

Secondly, the existence of a prostitute may provide a sexual outlet for young unmarried men who might otherwise attempt to seduce married women, with the possibility of wrecking established family units. This second function was recognized long ago by the ancient Greek authors. For example, Horace wrote: 'As soon as desire brings the blood in the veins of young men to boiling point, it is right and just that they should go this way and not seduce respectable married women.'

Prostitution was commonplace and widespread throughout the ancient world. Its value was recognized as a social service and brothels were conspicuously placed in many ancient cities, rather than being hidden away in dark corners. The great Mediterranean port of Ephesus, the ruins of which can be seen today in what is now western Turkey, had an extensive brothel in the very centre of the city. Amazingly, the brothel sign – surely the oldest in the world – has survived. It is in the form of an engraved paving slab, on which

*The quest for sexual novelty: in the US (top)
and Japan (above) there are many 'love
hotels' where loving couples can seek novel
sexual environments. For those who wish
to seek novel partners, almost every culture
has its 'ladies of pleasure' (left).*

are three images: on the right side is an image of a girl; in the middle is a footprint pointing in the direction of the brothel, and on the left side is a clearly marked pubic triangle, indicating what will be available once the visitor arrives there.

This liberal, open attitude towards prostitution – seeing it as a sexual safety valve –was not, however, to last. Religious piety was to sweep it away. Although Jesus is recorded as having been kind to a prostitute, Mary Magdalene, his ardent followers and the leaders of the Christian Church for centuries to come arrogantly ignored his gentleness and replaced it with ruthless suppression, insisting that all forms of sexual pleasure were the work of the devil.

All women, even respectable married ones, were inferior to all men in the eyes of these holy 'fathers', because women were more involved in the 'animalistic' aspects of human biology such as menstruation, birth and suckling. Men who enjoyed sex were a little better, and men who used sex reluctantly as a procreative duty were better still. Best of all, of course, were the celibate priests themselves, who eschewed all forms of reproductive activity. Needless to say, the prostitute, whose whole life was concerned with providing non-procreative sexual pleasure, came at the bottom of the social pile. As a result, prostitution and brothels were blacklisted and relegated to the social underground, where they have stayed ever since in almost every country in the world.

Despite these difficulties, the worldwide demand for this type of sexual service has never lessened. Even where it is totally illegal it somehow manages to flourish. Since the downfall of the Communist regime and the collapse of the repressive Soviet Union, it has become as familiar on the streets of Moscow as it is on the sidewalks of Los Angeles or the pavements of Paris. Many countries now turn a blind eye to it and, although it is still formally classified as illegal, make no attempt to enforce this. In a few countries there are even places where the authorities have decided to accept the inevitable and make prostitution safer by fully legalizing it.

In America, the state of Nevada first legalized brothel-keeping in 1967 and today there are no fewer than 36 licensed 'cathouses' in that state. Despite their legality and their official acceptance, they are mostly hidden away in isolated desert locations outside the cities to avoid stirring up puritanical opposition. They do, however, boast an *Official Guide to the Best Cathouses in Nevada*, which reads like a typical restaurant or hotel guide. In this it is recorded that, at one of the brothels – known as Cherry Patch II – there is a bizarre side-show in the form of a Prostitution Museum, complete with a display of brothel memorabilia including, in an open casket, 'Agnes, a mummified hooker who had stayed too long in the business'. Precisely how the presence of Agnes helps to improve the erotic atmosphere of this particular establishment is not explained.

Because of their uneventful success over three decades, these legal houses of prostitution have attracted the world of big business and plans were recently drawn up to construct the brothel to end all brothels, costing $130 million. It would take the form of a Polynesian resort on 300 acres near Las Vegas, complete with golf course, swimming pools, tennis and squash courts, car-racing track, private airstrip, 24 waterfalls and 12 ornamental gardens. The selection of the 500 resident prostitutes – women for male visitors and men for female visitors, to avoid criticisms of sexual bias – would require them to be both educated and multi-lingual. They would each earn about $10,000 a week. Visitors would pay an all-inclusive fee of $7000 for a weekend at the resort, during which they would be able to enjoy all the luxury facilities, including as many partners as they could manage.

Although this mega-brothel of the future plans to offer sexual gratification to both sexes, the vast majority of prostitutes worldwide are women. In brief, symbolic interludes, the male customers will act out their age-old urge to scatter their genetic material as widely as possible without embroiling themselves in more than one serious relationship. The primeval biological needs of the human male will demand expression; this has been the case for thousands of years and will probably always remain so.

Nonetheless, society will always remain ambivalent towards these activities, regardless of how legalized they become. Although they provide a valuable sexual service they also encourage pair-bond betrayal, and this will forever cloud their image.

For some men the casual affair, the long-term mistress and the short-time prostitute are not enough. Their urge to scatter their genetic material requires a more ambitious solution. They attempt the risky business of carrying on a number of major sexual relationships at one and the same time. Such men choose as their solution the condition known as polygamy.

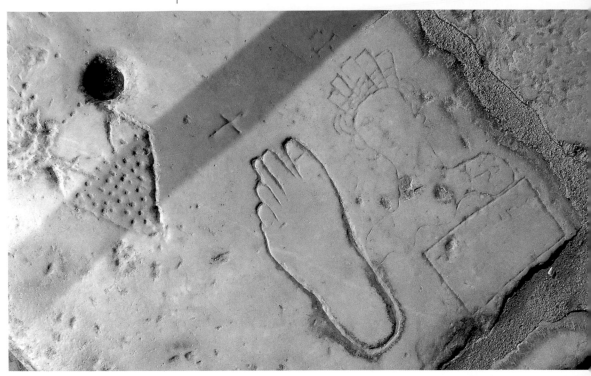

Polygamy

It is important to clear up a confusion that exists about the term polygamy, which means having more than one mate at any one time. It takes two forms: *polygyny*, in which a husband has more than one wife, and *polyandry*, in which a wife has more than one husband. Polygyny is widespread and common. Polyandry is extremely rare; in fact it is almost non-existent.

Polygyny has existed ever since human settlements became big enough to support rich, high-status males. If such men could afford to support more than one wife they were able to assemble harems of varying sizes. The problems they faced were: (1) jealousies and fights between the wives; (2) hostility from the frustrated males who were left without wives; and (3) the difficulty of controlling the sexual behaviour of a large number of women and preventing other males from 'stealing matings'.

The oldest brothel sign in the world, at ancient Ephesus, with a footprint pointing the way and a pubic triangle to indicate what was available (above). Inside this 2500-year-old brothel, an impressive phallic figure was found (below), confirming the building's function.

The risk of jealousies was reduced either by cruelty, through instilling abject fear into the harem wives, or by luxury, by making their lives so much better than anything they could hope for in the world outside the harem. Or both. Despite these tactics, the natural pair-bonding tendency of the human species did manage to assert itself in the form of endless status battles and squabbles between the wives. The result was that there was usually a senior wife and a number of junior ones. This arrangement was tantamount to one in which the harem-master was 'married' to the senior wife and carried on tolerated 'affairs' with the other wives.

The risk of hostility from the other males in the community who were effectively robbed of their female companions was almost always dealt with by tyranny and the imposition of fear. The risk of controlling the love-life of a large number of wives was handled by employing eunuchs to protect the harem quarters.

Many such harems existed during the course of history. The most famous, or infamous, was the harem at the Topkapi Palace in what is now the city of Istanbul. The Grand Seraglio of the great Turkish sultan was housed in palatial splendour, the women guarded, pampered and isolated from the outside world. The long history of this notorious harem was awash with plots and counter-plots, cruelty, torture and endless murders. The degraded behaviour of the people involved seems to confirm human polygyny as an unnatural state. But the position is not that simple. It has to be admitted that there have been – and still are – a number of multi-wife arrangements that work remarkably well.

In the Cameroons in West Africa, polygyny is commonplace. Men who are rich or powerful enough are able to collect together large groups of wives. One tribal leader, the powerful Fon of Mankon, a university graduate with a degree in agriculture who owns and runs a huge estate farming coffee and plantain, has over 70 wives and around 200 children. In addition to making true love-matches he also marries many wives as acts of charity. Whenever a male relative dies, for instance, he takes on the man's widow as his own responsibility, marrying her and caring for her, though not necessarily sleeping with her. Also, many of his children are adopted. He is, in the broadest sense, the father of his tribe. His social importance and his traditional authority enable him to act as an unquestioned, benign patriarch.

Perhaps the most colourful of all the Cameroon polygynists is the famous local pop star Mongo Faya. Idolized throughout the country, he is at present the proud husband of no fewer than 58 wives and the proud father of over 40 children. (He is uncertain of the exact number of offspring.) During his 43 years he has been through 80 marriage ceremonies and is already a grandfather. If other men have bedroom eyes, it could be said that Mongo Faya has dormitory eyes. It is his avowed ambition to build up his harem to a full 100 wives and to break his existing record of four marriages in one day. It all depends on how well his future hits climb the charts, for keeping such a large family is an expensive business.

His oldest wives are in their 40s, his youngest still in their teens. Some live with him together in a group. Others are scattered all over the country. He employs a certain degree of division of labour. There are several senior 'queen wives' who have special duties: for example, one is in charge of cooking, one is in charge of children and another leads his dance troupe. (He is probably the only pop singer who is married to his entire backing group). By giving each of his senior wives responsibility for one aspect of his life, Mongo Faya wisely reduces the risk of status clashes. And he takes the precaution of allowing all his existing wives (as represented by the queens) to approve of any new wife before a marriage can take place. They even have some say in who he sleeps with each night, although he may overrule them if he has a strong preference.

Describing himself as the King of the Faya Dynasty, Mongo maintains a formal dominance in his demeanour when in the presence of his wives. They must, for example, bow to him when entering the room. The combination of his glamour as a pop star, his fame as a healer and witch doctor, and his personal charisma, enable him to rule his huge family without resorting to pressure or threat. And there is a waiting list of young women eager to become one of his new brides.

In a country where poverty is common, Mongo's wives seem happy enough with this arrangement and the Faya clan appears to be a successful solution to the problem of how to establish an efficient family unit. There are only three clouds on the horizon. If Mongo's songs go out of fashion, what will become of his huge colony of dependent wives and children? Secondly, if his wives start to become jealous of one another, how will he be able to keep the peace? And finally, if all the other local males who have been denied even a single mate become frustrated, how will they react to his cornering the female market?

These may be distant clouds, but when they roll closer this happy harem may start to show its weaknesses and its inherent instability. Already cracks are beginning to appear. Recently, for example, 12 of his wives jointly sued him for divorce because the transportation arrangements he made for them were inadequate. Of his 80 wives, 22 have already left him and successfully sued for divorce. If more of his wives were to collude, they could turn their union with him into a disaffected wives' union and threaten to go on strike. Harem-masters must face the fact that they are riding a tiger. Only an exceptional individual as charismatic as Mongo can hope to keep a large collection of wives happy.

In many countries it is against the law for a man to have more than one wife. Problems then arise when particular religions allow such arrangements and therefore clash with legal ruling. In the United States, for example, certain states permitted polygyny for members of the Mormon Church until quite recently. Utah was one such state and, as a result, it became a centre for Mormon communities. Then, in the 1970s, Federal intervention saw the stamping out of polygyny in every state. There was then a brief period of persecution,

Polygyny. At the beautiful Palace of the Winds in Jaipur (left), each of the royal ladies had her own window from which she could watch the passing scene. In West Africa, the local pop singer, Mongo Faya (above) has already wed eighty times and is married to his entire backing group.

followed by indifference. Today Mormon men are left to live with their multi-partner groups if they so wish and the law turns a blind eye.

One such man is Alex Joseph. An ex-Mormon, he now refers to himself as a Political Christian and enjoys the company of eight wives, 26 children and 21 grandchildren. In purely evolutionary terms, his genetic line is growing rapidly and his genetic immortality is well assured. His attitude towards monogamy is that it is no more than a religious dictate from the Pope. He views all men who have remarried following divorce as having abandoned the state of monogamy. In other words, he sees no difference between simultaneous polygyny and serial polygyny.

How do the co-wives relate to one another when they are all present in the same house? The answer seems to be that they relish the division of labour, with each wife being able to specialize in those aspects of the married state that she most enjoys. Also, if one wife is feeling anti-social and wants to be alone for a while, she is able to do this without letting down her husband because there will always be other wives to turn to. In a monogamous relationship, they point out, the wife must be all things to her husband at all times. The co-wives can share these responsibilities, so there are fewer husband/wife conflicts.

Another co-wife bonus is a sense of security. If a man's 'second woman' is a secret lover or a mistress, such a partner is far less secure than a co-wife, whose status is assured. Shifty, dishonest, covert adultery is viewed as the Achilles' heel of monogamy.

The co-wives also insist that there are no feelings of jealousy because there is no sense of betrayal. The ground rules were laid down right from the start. Each one of then is, in a sense, monogamous – having only one man in their lives – and feels no different from other pair-bonded women. They are freer to pursue their careers or their preferred work, and when they do spend time with the man of the house it is time that is special and highly valued. However, it must be recorded that co-wives do admit to driving out unpopular wives when trouble occurs. The established women tend to gang up to protect themselves if newcomers threaten them. Although they have great respect for their shared male, they do not fit the sentimentally romantic picture of meek, pliant consorts obediently awaiting their master's pleasure. They have strength in numbers and their role is far from submissive.

In New York, among the black Muslims in Harlem, there is such a shortage of young males that the authorities have again turned a blind eye to the fact that most resident males have several wives. By Muslim law they are permitted four wives and many of them consider this teaching to provide a higher authority than that of the American government. The Federal Government, in its turn, sees the multi-wife arrangement as a satisfactory solution to the problem of how to care for a huge surplus of Muslim females, many of them with small, dependent children.

On the small islands of the South Pacific matters have always been more relaxed. If a man could afford more than one woman, nobody else seemed to object. On the island of Tahiti today there is a man called Pierre Tarahu, now in his 60s, who has gradually acquired 18 female partners who have given him a total of 67 children. Pierre's polygyny is the opposite of a harem. The essence of the harem is that the women are all kept together, shut away from the outside world and protected from the approaches of other males. Pierre's partners are scattered out far and wide all over the island and rarely meet one another. This eliminates any bickering or jealousies, but it does leave open the possibility of other males intruding.

Pierre's system operates as follows. When he has earned enough money he builds two houses. He then courts a woman and gives her both houses – one to live in, and one to rent. He visits her occasionally to make her pregnant and then leaves her to raise his children using the rent money obtained from the second house. When he can afford to build two more houses, he acquires another mate and repeats the process. So far he has built a total of 36 houses and has remained a happy and fulfilled man, doing the rounds of his extensive property holdings. What is perhaps most remarkable about him is that his job – the job that supports this elaborate domestic arrangement – is that of driving one of the service vehicles on the tarmac of Tahiti's international airport.

Surveying these different kinds of polygyny, the obvious question arises as to just how natural this mating system is for the human animal. There is a mass of evidence that supports the idea that human beings are essentially pair-forming and that other sexual systems are less appropriate. The undeniably heavy parental burden of the species demands that there should be an excessive amount of parental care available over a long period of time. The pair-bond offers the best hope of this. But clearly, under certain circumstances and with certain precautions, polygyny can work and can offer suitable parental care. Is it therefore an aberration that sometimes works under special circumstances, or a natural variation on the human breeding theme?

To find the answer one has to look at the nature of the relationships between the husband and each of his mates. Where society has conditioned males and females to convert their private sexual relationships into public status displays, these relationships have little emotional meaning. When love matches become arranged marriages or marriages of convenience, the feelings of a husband towards his wife or wives play only a minor role. The wives are seen purely as ways to amalgamate estates, or to provide some other economic benefit. Under these artificial conditions, the questions of falling in love or developing passionate attachments are of secondary importance. The human mating system has then become one that has more to do with expediency than with evolution.

Where this is not the case – where love is still paramount – the situation is more interesting. For the man involved there can be a separate, personal, loving response to each of his wives. It is as though he develops and maintains several pair-bonds simultaneously. For the women there are two problems: availability and jealousy. Where is he when they need him and who is he with? Availability is not such a problem if the man has sufficient power, wealth or thoughtfulness. He can provide substitutes for his own personal acts of caring. And in his favour is the fact that most monogamous males have to spend a great deal of their time away from their wives, earning a living. Against him is the thought that he, unlike the monogamous male, is away with another wife, sharing intimacies with her.

The main difficulty with sharing intimacies is that each truly loving relationship is based on total honesty. This means that, if wife number one tells her husband all her secrets, he must tell them all to wife number two or he will be keeping secrets from *her*. In other words, even if a polygynous male keeps his wives in separate houses to avoid jealous outbursts, he will nevertheless still be faced with controlling a complex network either of hidden knowledge or of betrayed confidences. In the end, this intensely personal, loving form of polygyny is deeply flawed. Only where marital relationships have been degraded to the level of business arrangements does it really stand a chance. But there it only works because the whole social structure is being forcibly held in place by powerful artificial controls. At best such controls cause endless repression, neurosis and lack of personal fulfilment; at worst, widespread misery.

It would appear then, that multi-wife arrangements will always be inadequate in some way, but it is only fair to mention an argument in their favour. This has been formally expressed by the Institute of Islamic Information, in defence of the one-husband/four-wife rule laid down by the Koran: 'Marry women of your choice, two, three or four...'

The Islamic authorities present the four-wife solution as a way of making men face up to their responsibilities. They accept that men will want to stray from any monogamous relationship and point out that, in a formally monogamous society, what happens is that each man has one 'public' wife and several other 'secret' women who are not treated with proper respect. By allowing him to marry these other women, Islam ensures that they too will be treated with proper respect as public wives.

Even the Koran has doubts about how well this will work in practice, however, as the full quotation reveals: 'Marry women of your choice, two, three or four; but if you fear that you shall not be able to deal justly with them, then only one...That will be more suitable, to prevent you from doing injustice.' Later, the point is made more strongly: 'You will never be able to deal justly between wives however much you desire to do so'.

The Islamic authorities sum up their official attitude by saying, 'Islam has allowed polygamy, limiting the number of wives to four, but does not require or even recommend polygamy'. (Note: by 'polygamy' here they mean only *polygyny*, because Islamic law forbids polyandry.)

Historically, it seems that the reason why Islam has allowed a multi-wife system is that Islamic peoples have so often suffered from the depredations of warfare and other forms of violence. These have decimated their male populations, leaving many females without mates. What becomes of the huge surplus of breeding females? The voice of Islam has little doubt about their fate: 'In a monogamous society these women, left without husbands or support, resort to prostitution, illicit relationships with married men resulting in illegitimate children with no responsibility on the part of the father, or lonely spinsterhood or widowhood.' So, to them, the four-wife rule provides a kind of social welfare system for surplus females.

Western women might view this rather differently. It is true that, even without wars raging, there is a large surplus of adult females. There are at present 8 million more women than men in the United States alone. Would these women be better off as co-wives? Islam only allows them three possibilities: whore, adulteress or pathetic loner. In reality, most of the surplus females in the West become career women (unthinkable to Islam), lesbians (equally unthinkable to Islam) or, if they do live alone, enjoy an active, outgoing social life (which also makes male-dominated Islam uneasy).

The fact is that if any society is going to support the concept of sexual equality, it must allow both forms of polygamy if it allows any. If a husband can show that he is able to support several wives, then a wife who can support several husbands should also be allowed to do so. It is unlikely that many women would be foolish enough to want to look after more than one husband, but the fact that Islam expressly forbids it, reveals its true colours. Like all major religions it treats women as essentially subordinate to men. Perhaps this is to be expected, since all important religious institutions today are run by elderly males who have little direct experience of women and whose personality types range from power-hungry to patronizing.

Polyandry: One Wife With Several Husbands

Up to this point only polygyny has been considered, but nothing has been said of its counterpart, polyandry. In fact, there is very little to say because, as mentioned earlier, it is virtually non-existent. Nowhere in the world is there the exact female equivalent of the male who has the pick of a group of females and nowhere can one find a culture where the normal arrangement is for each female to rule a harem of males.

In a survey carried out in 1949 of 238 widely different human cultures, it was discovered that many of them permitted some kind of polygyny, but that the figure for polyandry was below one per cent. In fact, there were only two polyandrous societies in the entire survey, and each of those had a special restriction.

One was the Toda of Southern India and the other was the Marquesans of Polynesia. Among the Toda, when a women married a man she also took on his brothers. She only had to go through one wedding ceremony, usually with the eldest brother, and from that point onwards she was automatically married to all his brothers, even ones that were not yet born. All the brothers had sexual access to the wife and the paternity of any child was arbitrarily decided by a simple ritual.

The reason for this unusual arrangement among the Toda was that their pastoral lifestyle benefited economically from keeping a group of brothers together as a social unit. This was not a case of the wife picking and choosing her mates, but rather a case of the bride being saddled with her groom's relatives whether she liked it or not. Since the men were all so close genetically, there was little 'genetic competition' between them, as regards fatherhood, and the system worked reasonably well. The co-husbands all occupied the one family house and the wife had her hands full carrying out the domestic chores for the whole group. To avoid clashes in the bedroom, a husband who was about to make love to the shared wife would hang his walking-stick outside the door, where it acted like an 'occupied' sign on a toilet.

According to a study made in the 1930s, the Marquesans of the South Pacific followed a slightly different mating pattern. Economic pressures were similar – there were severe droughts, crop failures and epidemics – and the wife needed several husbands to ensure the survival of her family. But the way she acquired her husbands was unique. She had a pair-bond with her main husband, who was the man who managed the family's affairs. In addition she had several other young husbands, selected from families of lower rank. These were 'junior' husbands and did not compete with the senior husband, to whom they were not related.

This Marquesan arrangement is very close to the situation seen in the West where a sexually energetic wife is fully pair-bonded with one particular male, but enjoys the sexual company of several younger men as secretive 'extras'. The difference is that, in the Marquesas, there was nothing secretive about the existence of these additional males.

A later study, reported in the 1960s, indicates that this arrangement had become little more than a cultural memory, stating bluntly: 'Polyandry is not found at present in the Marquesas'. It was even suggested that it never really existed in the first place, but this was essentially a matter of definition. If one accepts that to be truly polyandrous the wife must be *resident* with several husbands, then it is true that it never did occur. What happened was that the wife was monogamous and lived with only one man but was allowed to pay sexual visits to other men if she felt so inclined. This was called 'secondary mateship' and was not

Polyandry. The Toda people, Southern India, provide one of the rare examples of one wife having several husbands. In this culture, however, the husbands are always brothers (next page).

113

felt to represent true polyandry. After making two expeditions to study the sexual behaviour of the Marquesas islanders in the 1950s, anthropologist Robert Suggs concluded: '...that which was assumed to be polyandry in the Marquesas was, in fact, evidence of the widespread custom of secondary mateship, involving sexual access at irregular times, only upon permission of the primary spouse.'

Together, these studies of the Todas and the Marquesans virtually eliminate the 'wife-with-male-harem' as a valid human mating pattern. Female-controlled polyandry is not merely an extreme rarity, it is non-existent.

Non-Reproductive Sex

To sum up, the basic reproductive pattern of the human species appears to be monogamous, but with some degree of flexibility. This flexibility has made it possible for polygamous variations to occur, but these are usually flawed and unstable. In cases where they seem to work it is usually because they have become little more than 'masked monogamy' with a single, close, preferred partner and a number of minor, secondary ones.

In all reproductive patterns there are weaknesses. The strictly monogamous can so easily suffer the agony of betrayal. The powerfully polygamous can suffer from the chaos of pathological jealousies between the spouses. Everywhere there is the potential for domestic tension. Is there no alternative?

One drastic solution is to give up breeding altogether, forget the opposite sex – except as friends – and live a totally non-reproductive life. Someone taking this course of action could join a convent or a monastery, form a bond with someone of the same sex, join the Foreign Legion, or (in earlier days) go off on one of the Crusades.

The pious knights who, nine centuries ago, took off for the Holy Land to slaughter the infidels and save the world for Christ, had to swear an oath of celibacy. Those warrior monks – perhaps more correctly called 'Monkish Warriors' – were young aristocrats who answered the Pope's call for help in destroying the enemies of the Catholic Church. Their reason for espousing celibacy was that they had been indoctrinated with the idea that lovers, whether married or unmarried, were 'morally inferior to celibates'. In order to occupy the moral high ground that justified their Crusades they had to avoid the degrading, animalistic 'lust of the flesh'.

Originally the knights were all celibate, but as time passed most of them gave up their sacred vows. Today only one class of Knights is truly celibate – those called the Knights of Justice. They must still take a vow of chastity and live out their lives without family ties.

It is not clear how the original knights managed to satisfy their sexual urges. Perhaps they merely suppressed them, a condition of pent-up frustration that, back in the days of the Crusades, may have helped them to become emotionally more violent and hack non-Christians to pieces with a greater passion.

Many monks and nuns all over the world do seem to have managed somehow to suppress their sexual feelings and to endure a celibate lifestyle with at least an outward show of contentment. It is not clear how they sublimate their emotions. It is possible that they fail to do so rather more than they would have us believe, but this is something we will obviously never know.

For nuns there is a possibility of an emotional substitute for married life. They can undergo a ritual that marries them to Christ. As brides of Christ they may then be able to feel themselves in a spiritual form of pair-bond that may go some way to satisfy their deep-seated biological need to set up a family unit. By then engaging in nurturing, caring activities of various kinds they can also find an outlet for their frustrated maternal urges. But the manner in which they deal with their sexual longings remains a mystery.

The Catholic Church has shown itself to be deeply divided on the question of priestly celibacy. Those in favour of it have argued that it must be retained because of its 'spiritual values', because it enables priests 'to devote themselves to God with an undivided heart' and for the more practical reason that it 'prevents priests from passing Church property to offspring'. Those who wish to see it formally abandoned have also offered three reasons: it was not part of the original Church, there being married priests, bishops and even popes in the earliest days; its disappearance would 'reduce the incidence of paedophilia and homosexuality in the clergy'; and it would reduce the number of priests leaving the Church (during a recent 20-year period, 10,000 Italian and 20,000 American priests have left to get married).

The difference of opinion is easy to understand. On the one hand, by remaining celibate the priests avoid any family ties and any of the 'animalistic' aspects of human

A mass gay wedding ceremony in San Francisco, involving over 150 couples (next page).

reproduction. They devote themselves totally and exclusively to their religion. On the other hand, they must advise and counsel people on all matters, including sexual and parental activities of which they have no personal experience. There is a strange irony in the fact that they call themselves 'Father' when this is precisely what they are not.

Some sceptics find it hard to accept that healthy young adult males, whether priests or not, can survive month after month with a complete denial of any kind of sexual expression. Despite official pronouncements to the contrary, recent research tends to support this view. A 30-year investigation by an American author has revealed that, such is the intensity of the human sexual urges, at least half the supposedly virginal priests in the world fail to maintain their vows of celibacy. If this failure rate is true, the traditional image of the priest is seriously flawed.

An alternative form of non-breeding is one chosen by those who pair off with members of the same sex. Like monks and nuns, bachelors and spinsters, and pious knights, they belong to the non-breeding segment of society, but unlike those others they do not give up the comforts of paired sexuality.

In San Francisco recently, male/male and female/female couples took part in a mass wedding ceremony involving more than 150 couples. After each couple had been married they heard the words, 'By the virtue of the authority vested in me by the people of the City and County of San Francisco, I hereby pronounce you to be lawfully recognized domestic partners.' In every respect except the reproductive one they became monogamous family units. If they were to complete their mateship pattern by having children it would have to be by adoption or by some unorthodox means.

Some may query the necessity for such marriage ceremonies since, biologically, the individuals involved are not breeding units. If a same-sex couple are already living together as a 'pair', why go to the trouble of legalizing the relationship? The answer is that the motivation is more social and economic than biological. When a heterosexual couple weds, their marriage contract gives them no fewer than 170 advantages in the form of social rights, including social security benefits, pension payments, discounted memberships, visitation rights, medical decision-making, survivorship, immigration rights, disposal of community property and funeral rites. If one-sex pair-bonds are made official, homosexual couples could gain the same rights as heterosexuals in all these respects.

Wherever the illegality of such couplings has been removed it is only logical to take this next step.

In recent years there has been a continuing trend towards a general acceptance of same-sex pairings. There are still objections from some quarters – usually on religious grounds – but today in the West such partnerships are far less persecuted than they used to be. It is hard for us to comprehend the horror with which homosexual acts were greeted in earlier centuries. In parts of Europe in the sixteenth century, for example, the punishment for a man who was caught having sexual relations with another man was to be nailed by his penis to a stake for 24 hours in the city centre and then taken outside the city to be burned to death. By the eighteenth century, however, Thomas Jefferson had suggested reducing the punishment for sodomy from the death penalty to castration, while in the British Royal Navy the punishment for buggery was sometimes reduced to a 'mere' 1000 lashes.

By the early part of the nineteenth century we read of a police raid on a homosexual club in London, following which some of those arrested were sent to jail for three years. Although this is a far less severe punishment, it was only imposed after the men had been put on public display in the pillory, where they were forced to submit to having mud, eggs and dead cats thrown at them. By the end of that century, in the infamous sodomy trial of Oscar Wilde, there was a sentence of two years' hard labour but the humiliation of the public pillory had gone.

During the twentieth century the hostile attitude towards homosexual acts gradually softened. Today it is more widely accepted as an alternative lifestyle and, in the West at least, formal punishments have become a rarity. There is a simple reason for this. As human populations have become increasingly overcrowded, society has unconsciously relaxed its antagonism to those who wish to set up non-breeding families. If the population were suddenly to be decimated, attitudes would rapidly change and non-breeding would once again come under savage attack. But the certain knowledge that today we are horribly overpopulated makes it possible for those who wish to turn to this form of non-reproductive sexual expression to be accepted by the rest of society. Like monks, nuns, bachelors, spinsters and all the other non-breeders, they are welcome non-populators.

One of the problems faced by those who engage in sex with their own gender is the inevitable incompleteness of their sexual sequence. For many individuals, because the sequence cannot reach its biological climax – of pregnancy and birth – there is a tendency to keep on repeating the earlier parts of the sexual sequence. In other words, the courtship phase becomes a behavioural loop that goes round and round, with one sexual conquest following another. Even when a relationship manages to get past the initial phase and a male/male couple does set up home as a pair, there is a greater chance that it will be disrupted and break apart, simply because there are no children stemming from the sexual intimacies to complete the reproductive pattern. This is as true for female/female interactions as it is for male/male ones. The initial phases of the sexual sequence are much more in evidence and much more repeated than with heterosexual couples.

Another problem faced by female/female pairings is the absence of a penetrating organ. There are, of course, other ways of achieving sexual excitement. Clitoral stimulation can go a long way towards satisfying female sexual cravings, but penetration of one partner by another remains a rather basic element in any human sexual relationship. The clitoris may provide endless orgasms, but the deep psychological need for the ultimate intimacy of sexual penetration also demands its own kind of satisfaction and there are those who have built an industry on consummating this primeval urge. A visit to any dildo factory, where penetration is mass produced, will verify this.

Solitary Sex

If there are problems with monogamy, polygyny, polyandry, celibacy and homosexuality, then what is left? The answer for many is solitary sex. Sex without contact. It avoids domestic fighting, it avoids messy divorce proceedings, it avoids pious frustrations and it avoids Aids. It is little wonder that it has recently become increasingly popular.

Indeed, solitary sex has become big business. A 1995 catalogue of sex toys published in San Francisco listed no fewer than 120 different models, ranging from such intriguing inventions as the Wonder Wand, the Emerald Twister and the Rabbit Pearl to the Double Daisy, the Triple Ripple and the Pocket Rocket. Most of these toys are little more than glorified dildos, but some of them reflect a new ingenuity on the part of the manufacturers who, judging by their frenetic inventiveness, must think that they are catering to a somewhat jaded clientele. The Hummingbird, for example, is an electrically vibrating G-string.

The brochure explains that, 'Two vibrating bullets are tucked inside the soft vinyl body of the Hummingbird, each controlled by a separate switch on the variable-speed battery pack.' Or there is the Leather Butterfly, complete *Solitary sex: the sex show where visitors, peeping through small windows, can see but not touch.*
with an electrically-operated vibrating egg, that can be worn invisibly by a woman while enjoying a candlelit dinner.

These remarkable devices are all marketed under the banner of safe sex with proclamations such as, 'How to have safe, fun sex in the 90s'. The catalogue enthuses about its extraordinary products with a cosy friendliness: 'Many people's sex lives have been affected by concern about sexually transmitted diseases. The good news is that you can have safe sex with all of the toys in our catalog…they're affordable, practical and fun.'

It was Salvador Dali, the Spanish Surrealist, who foreshadowed the modern obsession with solitary sex when he wrote his only novel, *Hidden Faces*, in 1944. In this tale he invented what he called his own personal perversion. He called it Cledalism, after Cleda, the heroine of his novel. Cledalism consisted of two people being able to reach simultaneous orgasm without touching one another. Ultimately they were able to do this without even being in the same room with one another. This is merely a Dalinian exaggeration of what happens in every pornography establishment in the world, where one sex comes to gawp at the other without making contact.

For men who watch pornographic displays, the thrill of these encounters is to see but not touch. They enjoy the pleasures of sexual arousal without any form of sexual commitment. After their encounters they can disappear back into their private worlds without personal embroilments or complications. It is sex with a minimum of involvement. Through the medium of sex shows, sex films and sex magazines, this type of erotic fulfilment has become increasingly widespread in recent years. It is as if we are entering an era of extreme sexual interest held in check by extreme sexual caution.

The ultimate form of solitary sex is now available via the internet. Interactive sex with a distant partner is possible through the magic of the modern computer. Salvador Dali would have relished this as a modern form of Cledalism. The female sits alone in a room on the other side of the world. The male calls up her number and pays her fee by credit card; she then appears on the screen and responds to whatever request he taps on to his keyboard. Sex can never become more remote than this.

The Pair-Bonding Species

In the end, after contemplating all the different types of mateship system known to mankind, it is hard to see one that is perfect, but there can be no denying that, given half the chance, we are as a species biologically programmed to fall in love and form pairs. And that these pairs are the basis for future breeding, without which, of course, the human animal would soon disappear.

However, although this simple system lies at the heart of human reproduction, evolution has not made it 100 per cent binding, because to become completely fixated on a sexual partner, who might die young, would be biologically wasteful. The system has to retain a degree of flexibility to avoid this. And it is this built-in flexibility that can then lead to many of the problems we know so well.

Sometimes, however, the bonds of love are so immensely powerful that this flexibility is suppressed. Young wives continue to mourn their departed husbands long after all hope for them is lost. Some women may never recover from the loss of a loved one; for others it may take years. This is poignantly illustrated by tragic scenes that can be observed outside the Kresty Prison in St Petersburg. Inside the ugly walls of that forbidding establishment are men who have been condemned to die for serious crimes they have committed. They are penned in, 16 to a cell which has only four beds, and must take it in turns to sleep. In these inhuman conditions they have only one thought – to see their loved ones for one last time. To do this they laboriously remove a brick from their heavily shuttered windows and then somehow manage to angle a small shaving mirror on a stick out into a position where they can see their wives' images reflected in it.

The pathetic wives come each day to stand on the street outside the prison, sending visual signals of love to the partners they will never see or hold in their arms again. Occasionally, the men manage to dispatch small paper messages, in the form of rolled up darts shot through a makeshift blowpipe. The messages fall to the ground on the busy road and their wives rush into the passing traffic to pick them up.

The men in the lower cells are unable to perform this blowpipe communication, but they are helped by the prisoners in the upper windows, who let down fishing lines to which messages can be attached. These are then reeled in and dispatched by blowpipes from the upper windows.

What is happening outside Kresty Prison is ample proof of the intensity of the emotional attachments that exist between individual males and females. For the Russian couples involved there is no possibility of further family life, no possible future for husband and wife as a breeding unit. The situation for these men and women is completely without hope. They will never be together again and yet their passion for one another refuses to die. After the men have been executed and the years have passed, perhaps then the women may be emotionally capable of starting up new relationships. But in the meantime, the power of human love continues to express itself in this moving way.

The human pairing system may have its weaknesses but it also has its amazing strengths, regardless of the obstacles that modern urban life throws at it. And until our species has either exterminated itself completely, or has evolved onto an entirely new plane, it will always be so.

4

Passages of Life

Today the human animal lives longer than any other species of land mammal. Our life span is so long that we try to divide it up into segments. We create helpful punctuations in our life sentence. We speak of childhood, adolescence, middle age, old age and senility. Increasingly, we see ourselves as belonging to one of these major phases of life, and we create special events to mark our passage from one stage to the next. These rites of passage frequently help us to reaffirm and reinforce our masculinity or femininity. Even when gender plays a secondary role in these ceremonies it may nevertheless make a considerable impact.

By nature, these rites of passage are extremely localized in their significance. Although everyone can understand the general meaning of each event, the smaller details of the procedure are frequently meaningless to all but the people directly involved. Each culture has its own legends and traditions, symbols and beliefs. These are woven together to magnify the psychological 'weight' of an event and to make it as impressive and awe-inspiring as possible for the participants. What is sombrely important for them may appear to be no more than superstitious mumbo jumbo to outsiders. It is worth remembering, though, that other cultures must also view our own most sacred ceremonies as equally preposterous when gazed upon from their distant position.

The Primeval Feast

Although today we have all kinds of ceremonies for all kinds of occasions, the earliest and most ancient of all our celebrations must have been the feast, the feast that took place following a successful hunt. Before our early ancestors became hunters, their lives will have lacked the great moment, the special event, but once we began to pursue big game our whole lifestyle changed.

Males set off on the chase while females stayed behind

The primeval feast, still enjoyed today by tribal communities (above), must have been the most ancient of all human rituals. It is now so ingrained in human nature that it resurfaces in many forms (below), even when feeding is not the central focus of the occasion.

near the camp site. When the men returned, there was a triumphant gathering in which the whole tribe participated. These feasts provided peak moments in the human life cycle and created the template for other, more varied ceremonies and events that were to develop at a much later date. This is why at so many of our modern events we include food and feasting, even if, as at a wedding reception, eating is not really relevant to the activities at the centre of the celebration.

At most of these ceremonies, being male or female has a special significance. The ritual actions we perform, and the costumes we wear, help to give each of us a stronger gender identity. The nature of the events often serves to make males more masculine and females more feminine. At a wedding, the bride and groom appear in strongly contrasting costumes, probably as different from one another as they will ever be in their entire lives. Tomorrow they may both be wearing jeans and T-shirts, but today their gender displays are polarized.

The New Arrival

In some countries the typical wedding ceremony is followed by another, less familiar ritual. In Estonia, near the Russian border, a newly married couple, accompanied by their wedding guests, visit a sacred tree. They believe that, if the groom climbs high into this tall tree and ties a ribbon on one of its upper branches, the action will encourage the early and successful birth of a child. The higher the groom goes, the better his bride's chances of becoming pregnant quickly. And if they have a preference for a boy or a girl, they can influence this by the colour of the ribbon he uses – pink for a girl or blue for a boy.

The arrival of the newborn is a time for ceremony in almost every culture. It would seem reasonable to suppose that a successful birth would demand a ceremony that is also a celebration, but matters are more complicated than that. In the primeval forest the act of giving birth is seen as simple and perfectly natural, but once society has become more complex and is dominated by a powerful male priesthood it may lose its simple character. In pious patriarchal eyes, giving birth becomes somehow bestial and faintly disgusting.

In parts of Greece, for instance, the mother is considered impure after she has given birth and is confined for 40 days. During this phase she must stay in her home and is not allowed to enter a church or take part in religious services. At the end of her confinement she must attend a special ceremony to mark her return to the fold. Amazingly, Greek women, even today, are prepared to accept this form of humiliation. The origins of this curious ritual can be traced to the Old Testament, where it was categorically stated that a woman shall be unclean for 40 days after giving birth and shall 'touch no hallowed thing, nor come into the sanctuary, until the days of her purifying be fulfilled'. After the 40 days are over she has to make an animal sacrifice, after which the priest will 'make atonement for her and she will be cleansed from the fountain of her blood'.

The central theme here is female bleeding. This is seen by a male-dominated religion as defiling, presumably because it is a vivid reminder of humanity's animal nature. The fact that men's bodies are not required to perform the bloody business of giving birth places them further from the animals and therefore closer to God. This superstitious nonsense – converting the act of giving birth from a wondrous natural event into a disgusting bestial necessity – was just one of the many ways in which a devious male priesthood sought to reduce all women to an inferior status.

Not long after entering the world, the newborn is given its own special gender display in the form of pink or blue clothing. This tradition of blue for a boy and pink for a girl can be traced back to ancient times when a male offspring was considered to be a much greater asset than a female addition to the family. The blue colour was thought to be protective, and the male baby needed all the protection it could be given. Blue was seen as the colour of heaven, and therefore the colour that would repel the evil forces that were inevitably attracted to the innocent newborn baby. To the superstitious, adorning the baby with blue colours was a defensive act that would keep it safe in a world full of malevolent spirits. In some countries, simply clothing the baby boy in blue was not enough. Blue ornaments had to be hung in the rooms and it was even necessary to paint the front door of the dwelling a bright blue.

The female newborn did not receive such protective treatment. She needed a display colour that would distinguish her from the male baby. And the chosen colour was pink, symbolizing her biological colour – at least in the countries where this tradition grew up.

Among the Yemen, the arrival of a baby boy is celebrated with a special feast for the mother and her female friends. Male babies are always favoured. Here, the baby boy is decorated with protective signs, but the baby girl is not. (next page).

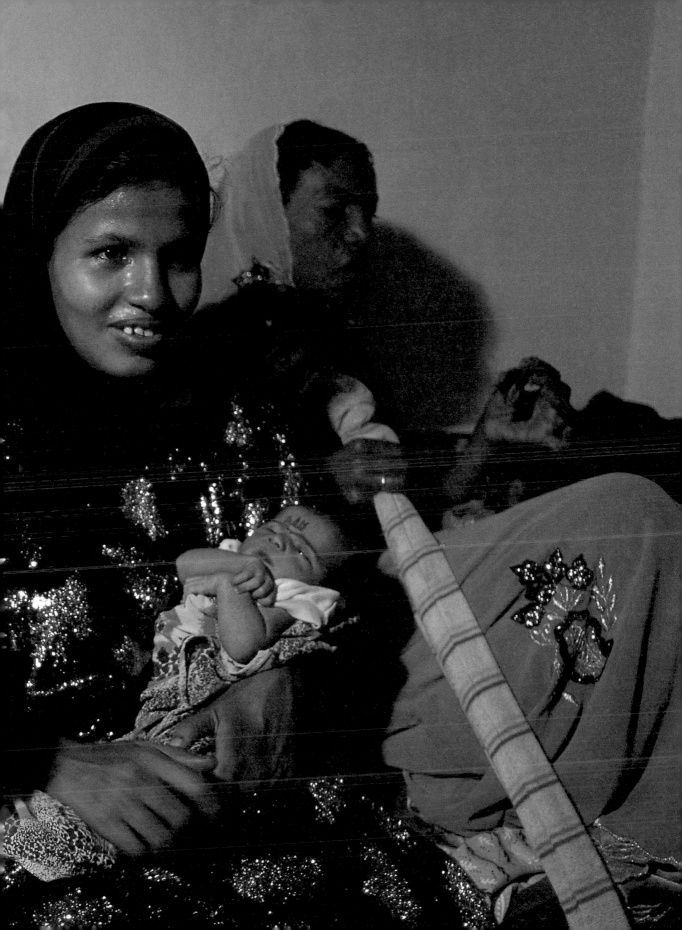

As soon as possible the baby had to be given further protection by contact with holy water. It was believed that the newborn was so attractive to evil spirits that they would rush to greet it and enter its body, taking control of it for the rest of its life. The only solution was to cleanse it with sacred water that would repel the evil ones. If boys and girls were brought to a baptism together, it was therefore vital for the boys to be baptized first so that no time would be wasted in giving them this extra defence against the forces of evil.

In some warring countries there was a further gender difference. A male baby had his right arm kept carefully dry during his baptism ceremony. This was to ensure that he would grow up pure in heart, but evil in his right arm – the limb that would become his adult weapon of death and destruction.

As part of this ritual of cleansing by water it was also important to label the gender of the baby by giving it a name, with the chosen names nearly always being gender specific.

In Greece, a special distinction is made between boy and girl babies at the time of baptism. Only boys are permitted to be taken into the sanctuary of the church. When it arrives at the church, the baby is anointed with oil and then immersed three times in the font of the central part of the church. After this, if the baby is a boy, he is carried by the priest through the royal doors and into the sanctuary. If the baby is a girl, she is carried to the doors, but is not allowed to pass through. From the very start of their social lives, under the influence of the male-dominated priesthood, these little children are being treated differently, and each cultural ceremony underlines this fact.

In the Yemen, for example, the birth of a baby boy is celebrated with a special feast and a party when he is three days old. All the female friends of the new mother gather at her house, remove their veils and plunge their right hands into large bowls of food. In addition to the feasting, the women hang garlands of jasmine around the mother's neck, enjoy a shared smoke with a water-pipe and make money offerings to the infant. The baby boy is protected during the ceremony by a special pattern painted in black kohl on his forehead and by a copy of the Koran placed close to his body. When a baby girl is born, there is no such celebration.

All over the world, different cultures have some way of commemorating the arrival of the newborn. This induction of the child into society is an important way of saying 'we accept this child and it is now one of us'. In certain parts of Pakistan, for example, both the mother and her new baby must be blessed by a girl who is herself a virgin. The virgin's own purity is thought to purify the new arrival. Once again, the concept of the virgin as pure and the breeding woman as somehow impure is employed as a cultural insult to the mother and to her all-important act of procreation. Biologically it would make more sense to label the virgin as impure, since she has not yet fulfilled her major reproductive role.

In some countries where child mortality was high there used to be a special ceremony when an infant reached its first birthday. In certain regions of the Mediterranean this ceremony still takes place, even today. On the small island of Malta it is known as *Il-Quccija*. The relatives and friends of the family gather at the parents' home to celebrate the fact that the infant has successfully passed through the dangerous first year of life and has completed its babyhood. But there is more to the ceremony than a celebration, for this is a moment when the child's future will be decided, or at least suggested. A tray of small objects is carried in and placed on the floor. The birthday baby is then put down on the other side of the room and allowed to crawl about in any direction it likes. Watched by family and guests it starts to explore, moving this way and that until, eventually, it comes upon the tray. Seeing the array of interesting objects, it reaches out and picks one up. Its choice of object is considered to have great significance and is used to predict its future role in life.

The traditional objects employed in this little ceremony include an egg, a pen, some coins, a ball, rosary beads and scissors. If the infant picks up the egg, there will be an abundance of happiness; if the pen, a desk job; if the coins, wealth; if the rosary beads, the Church; if the ball, sport; if the scissors, tailoring.

Other, additional objects offered are gender specific. If the infant is a boy there will probably be something connected with his father's trade or profession. An electrician might place a small electrical appliance there; an architect would include something from his drawing board, a painter a paint brush, and so on. Fathers often hope fervently that the child will pick up such an object and will then be more likely to carry on the family business tradition. (Some over-enthusiastic fathers have been known secretly to rehearse their infant sons, encouraging them to play with their preferred object so that when the great day comes they will go straight to it. Unfortunately, this has little impact because the sheer novelty of the other, unfamiliar objects may draw the child towards them instead.)

133

If the infant is a girl, there will be more feminine objects placed on the tray to choose from. By pre-selecting the offered objects in this manner, the choices can be narrowed down slightly and the child's future direction can be guided towards an appropriately masculine or feminine pursuit. In this way, the ceremony acts as another step in the long cultural process of indoctrinating a child into its life-long gender role.

After the dramas of birth and baptism, a child's ordeals are far from over. In many cultures the children must face the ritual genital mutilation we call circumcision. This extraordinary procedure which, were it not hallowed by ancient tradition, would be prosecuted as child abuse, occurs in several forms in different parts of the world, some-times applied to young males and sometimes to young females. In all cases parts of the external genitals are removed — the foreskin in males and the clitoris and/or labia in females. Male children are usually mutilated by older males and female children by older females.

Literally millions of cases of these genital assaults occur annually and a whole range of preposterous excuses and explanations have been given as to why this savaging of young humans is necessary. In earlier days most of the explanations had to do with religious dictates, sacred demands that could not be queried rationally. With the fading of religious beliefs in some countries in later years, new excuses had to be found and a set of spurious medical reasons were invented.

In origin, male circumcision is an ancient Egyptian custom employed to ensure immortality. The snake sheds its skin and becomes renewed, seemingly immortal. So, if a human male sheds a piece of skin he too will become immortal. The Egyptians also noticed that the kind of baboon that they called sacred was 'born circumcised' and concluded from this that the uncircumcised condition must signify someone who is lacking in sacred qualities. This curious custom spread from Egypt to other cultures in the Middle East, and from there around much of the world.

In many cultures, male circumcision is performed within weeks of the birth. The Jewish faith calls for circumcision on the eighth day following the birth. The baby suffers acute pain, but is otherwise uninvolved in the ritual. In some countries, however, the mutilation is deferred until the male children are fully aware of what is going on. In Turkey, for instance, boys are usually circumcised between the ages of three and nine years.

Frequently there are mass circumcisions, carried out in a party atmosphere. A clown is sometimes employed to distract the nervous children. One famous knife-wielder, nicknamed the 'The Sultan of Circumcision', has been known to perform as many as 2000 operations in a single day.

In modern Turkey, the ritual of male circumcision is carried out when boys are between the ages of three and nine years.

When a boy is selected, his mother may not intervene. He is held down by his godfather while his foreskin is cut away. Afterwards he is given a diploma and must kiss the hand of the man who has mutilated him. He is then handed back to his anxious mother, who comforts him. When all the boys have been done there is a great celebration with music and dancing.

The spread of female circumcision has been less successful and it is still limited largely to Africa and the Middle East. The reason for this form of child mutilation is more obvious, that is, to reduce the sexual pleasure of the female when she becomes adult and therefore make her less likely to be unfaithful to her husband. The official excuse sometimes given is that the removal of the external female genitals makes women less 'animalistic'.

No other species behaves in this bizarre way towards its young, but where religious customs take a hold on a culture it is usually difficult to shift them. No matter how cruel or pointless they may be, they become stubbornly resistant to common sense or objective medical opinion.

In recent years a rebellion against male circumcision has been gaining momentum. A book with the startling title of *The Joy of Uncircumcising* has been published by a Californian professor of psychology, who recommends the replacement of the lost foreskin by prolonged skin-stretching techniques. Weights and tapes are attached to the circumcised penis over long periods of time, gradually stretching the skin down to cover the tip. The technique is based on the principle of tissue expansion, which is well known in reconstructive surgical procedures. It takes several years for the skin to expand enough to cover the glans, but men who have persisted with the treatment report that, eventually, the replacement of the foreskin is successfully achieved. Use of this replacement technique has now spread from America to Europe, where hundreds of men are laboriously attempting to undo the damage caused by the genital rituals of childhood. For circumcised women there is no such hope of replacement. Once the labia and clitoris have been removed, their sensitive sexual skin is gone for ever.

Childhood Gender Separations

In many modern societies where children leave home to receive formal educations, there are further gender rituals that separate the boys from the girls. Although some schools and colleges are co-educational and enjoy a relaxed dress code, many others are unisexual and uniformed. The dress codes mark out boys as boys and girls as girls. In a hundred small ways the young males and young females have their gender roles reinforced, not only by the school authorities but also by their own actions. Male language, slang, gesture, posture, play and preoccupation all come to differ markedly from the behaviour displayed by young females.

In the learning years between five and 15 – sometimes called the 'blotting-paper years' because schoolchildren in this age group are so receptive to massive mental input – there is an increasing tendency for the two sexes to split apart. The male world and the female world develop in different directions. Male gangs and female groups proliferate and help to keep the gender gap as wide as possible. This is the valuable calm before the sexual storm of adolescence. It is valuable because it turns the opposite sex into a group of comparative strangers; strangers who can then be rediscovered in an entirely new context when sexual maturity arrives.

Rituals of Puberty

As soon as the growing child develops sexual characteristics – female breasts, male beard, female hips, male voice – there are special events that mark out this important new phase of life.

Each society has its own way of welcoming newcomers to the sexually active arena. In some, the moment is warmly celebrated. The new adults are congratulated on reaching adulthood and are given some kind of social 'label' to identify them as having come of age. This may be a special form of clothing. In the West, among young males, it used to be the wearing of the first 'grown-up' suit. This involved the conspicuous shift from short trousers to long trousers – and it still does in certain parts of society.

Although obeying an unwritten rule, this clothing change followed fairly strict lines. A young boy wearing long trousers or a fully adult male wearing short trousers would have been the butt of jokes and would be looked upon as ridiculous. The same was true of girls wearing bras. Worn on flat-chested little girls, or not worn on full-busted adults, the bra became a source of humour. More recently, fashions have changed, so much so that such hard-and-fast rules no longer apply to a large part of the population. With a more liberated society there is far less interest in fixed rites of passage.

In countries with a greater respect for tradition, there is usually a ceremony to mark the coming of age. Throughout Latin America, for instance, there is a Catholic ritual called the *Quinceanera* (pronounced keen-se-an-yeh-ra), which takes place on the occasion of a girl's 15th birthday. She is 'queen for a day' and dresses in an elaborate, formal costume similar to a bridal dress. The event celebrates both her physical innocence and her arrival on the threshold of womanhood. In other words, her surviving virginity and the imminence of its loss.

The event begins with a mass in church and ends with a huge dinner party – a family fiesta with music and dancing. In occurs even in North America, wherever Hispanic

populations are large enough. In Houston, for example, where more than 30 per cent of the local population is Hispanic, it is widely celebrated and is popularly known as 'The Quince'. Formally, it is the occasion for reaffirming baptismal vows and for expressing a commitment to chastity before marriage. Informally, it is a rite of passage in which family ties are strengthened, both internally between the members of the family and externally between the family and the rest of society.

Coming-of-age rituals take many forms. In Latin America (above) a girl celebrates her fifteenth birthday at a Quinceanera ceremony, when she is 'queen for a day'. In the Yemen (right), a boy becomes a man when he is presented with his first adult male dagger.

The displays of 'The Quince' last for only one day, but in countries with a more rigid social structure the emblem of the coming-of-age ritual is more permanent. It remains on show from that moment on, and involves every male or every

female, without exception. In the Yemen, for instance, with males, this display involves the wearing of an adult dagger, or *djambia*. Boys wear toy daggers, but when they reach the age of 12 they are taken by their fathers to buy their first serious, adult dagger. This is then proudly worn on the young man's belt and carried with him at all times.

In addition to showing his age, the *djambia* also transmits signals concerning the wearer's social status. The higher his status, the more expensive will be the dagger handle. Top males are only satisfied with an unbelievably expensive rhino-horn handle, a status display so intense that it has nearly exterminated the African rhinos. There are two other status signals available to the dagger-wearing male: for high status, it is worn nearer the hip; for low status, nearer the crotch. Another indicator of high status is to wear it at an angle, while for low status it is worn vertically. There is nothing to stop a male from cheating and changing the angle of his dagger, but he does not do this because everyone would know he was cheating and the strategy would lose its value.

Young females in the Yemen greet their puberty by buying their first veil. As children they can show their face to the world because they are too young to become active brides. But once they experience their first menstruation everything changes. They must now cover their bodies completely and remain in this state until they are married. Even then, they are only allowed to unveil themselves and show their faces in private, in the company of their husbands or female intimates.

Young Yemeni adolescents are the lucky ones. Their coming-of-age is a pleasant celebration. But in other cultures the situation is very different. There, it is a time for unpleasant ordeals, as though the adults somehow resent the rise of a new generation beneath them that pushes them one step further away from their own youthful condition. In many societies this unease among the adults is hidden behind polite phrases. The ordeals of initiation are explained away as important labelling devices, special honours to be hard won or badges to be worn proudly to announce the new, reproductive condition of the youngest adults in the community.

In some cultures, this adult displeasure at being shunted on to a less youthful condition is more overt. Among the Mursi of Ethiopia, the hostility of the older generation is blatantly obvious, and indeed constitutes the basis of their tribal puberty ritual. When young Mursi boys reach sexual maturity their 'welcome' to adult life consists of a violent beating by their tribal elders. They are pursued and whipped by older men who, when questioned about their violent actions, openly admit that they are attacking the boys because they are 'stealing' their adult status.

Although few cultures are this honest about their rites of passage, it is nevertheless clear that the essence of many puberty rituals is the humiliation of the newly matured generation. The ingenuity of human adults in finding unpleasant ways to torment the newcomers is remarkable. The official excuse is usually simply that a particular ordeal is 'steeped in tradition'. This is supposed to be sufficient explanation to satisfy the frightened youngsters who then permit themselves to be subjected to painful tooth-filing, scarification, tattooing or some other form of bizarre mutilation.

No other species of animal behaves in this way. Puberty ordeals are uniquely human and, it has to be said, not one of our more attractive features. As highly intelligent primates, one might expect us to devise something more celebratory. The new generation of human beings, if fit and healthy, represents a reproductive triumph that should be a cause for great rejoicing. Instead, it is all too often greeted with brutal ceremonies inspired by ill-concealed envy. The initiations are formally presented as procedures born of adult experience and superiority – the adults possessing the mysterious 'knowledge' of what must be done to the young to make them true men or women – but in reality the events are spawned by the adult fear of being superseded and becoming obsolete.

Although advanced societies today have managed to curb most of these humiliating practices, they have in the process acquired a new puberty challenge of their own. Our modern, technologically sophisticated cultures have become so complex that it now takes nearly a decade for young *biological* adults to mature into young *social* adults. The gap between these two thresholds – between the age at which the young acquire sexual maturity and the age at which they are ready to marry and set up a family home – creates its own special problems. How does a society contrive to delay the course of nature?

The facts are these: by the time they are 14, 80 per cent of girls will have started to menstruate; by the same age, 90 per cent of boys will have experienced their first ejaculation. In other words, at the very start of the teenage period the vast majority of young human males and females are ready to breed. Yet the favourite age for getting married is years away. In the United States, the most popular age for a young woman to be married is

20; for a young man it is 23. In the UK, the figures are 20 and 24. So there is an average gap of six years for a girl and 10 years for a boy.

In theory, this period of time – the very time when human sexuality is at its freshest and most intense – is meant to be virginal and celibate. In an idealized scenario the young bride and groom lose their virginity on their wedding night. In practice, this rarely happens. Most teenagers have discovered the joys of sex long before they utter their quaintly archaic marriage vows. Society pretends to ignore their informal acquisition of carnal knowledge, and does its best to prevent the situation from getting out of hand.

The impact of this adult charade on the adolescent population can be disastrous. Forced into the shadows, many of the earliest sexual experiences are riddled with shame, clumsiness, ignorance and fear, when they should in fact be amongst the most joyous experiences of an entire lifetime. The sexual rite of passage for the young adults of advanced cultures is more likely to be a furtive rather than a festive affair.

Authorities complain bitterly that there is little they can do about this because the social skills needed in order to become established as a viable adult in modern urban society are such that nobody is ready to face the world as an independent citizen until they are into their 20s. The teenage period must remain a phase of acute frustration or secretive pleasure.

There are two ways of handling this dilemma: freedom with trust, or ruthless isolation. In the West, freedom is the general rule. Teenagers are allowed out to play, so to speak, with the forlorn hope that their games will not be too adult. A whole subculture of adolescent pursuits is developed which, it is supposed, will preoccupy them. Advanced education is made as demanding as possible to absorb more of their time and energy. Stern warnings concerning venereal diseases, Aids and the risks of pregnancy are given. Just in case all these measures fail, information about contraception and safe sex is offered as a last-ditch precaution.

Despite all this, the biological urges are so powerful that many young couples throw caution to the wind and celebrate their newly acquired physical condition in private rituals of lust and love. For the teenage boys, the experience gained may prove to be valuable, so that by the time they reach their major rite of passage – their wedding day – they will be sufficiently experienced sexually to avoid any damaging clumsiness with their brides. For

the teenage girls, the matter is more serious. Huge numbers of them become pregnant long before they can establish a family home.

Schoolgirls with babies. In the West, where teenagers have more freedom, it is not always easy to postpone the reproductive process.

For many girls this creates a traumatic situation, with society preferring to sweep them under the social carpet and forget them. But some cities, both in the United States and Europe, have begun to take a more positive attitude. Specialist schools have been set up where teenage mothers can attend classes and continue with their education while at the same time acting as fulfilled young mothers, lovingly rearing their children. Within these schools, special rooms are made available for breast-feeding between classes and the adolescent mothers are also given as much help as possible in caring for their young ones.

Instead of attaching a stigma to these young females and rejecting them as pariahs, they are treated with respect as the young mothers of a future generation. They will inevitably face a heavier burden than usual as young adults and need all the help they can get. These new specialist schools, of which there are still far too few, offer them just that. There was nothing unnatural about their sexual appetites. What was unnatural was society's attempt to make them mark time for so long. If society fails to do this, the appropriate response is to offer sensitive assistance rather than to ostracize or castigate.

The alternative is ruthless isolation. Where it occurs, this is usually only applied to the young females – the ones more at risk from early sexual encounters. In previous centuries teenage girls were often shut away in unisex schools, regimented by rigidly authoritarian teachers and generally reduced to the level of uniformed learning machines. Where such methods were applied they either crushed the spirits of the girls concerned or alternatively created fiery, frustrated rebels impatiently awaiting their delayed moment of wild abandon.

In some tribal societies the degree of isolation of young females is astonishing and makes even a convent school seem liberated. In the Wayuu culture in South America, a young female is shut away as soon as she has experienced her first menstruation. Her confinement may last for up to three years, during which time she is taught the traditions of her tribe and learns how to weave. Working in a small hut she is expected to make elaborate hand-woven hammocks, each of which would take her about eight months to complete. During this time she is not allowed to speak to any male of any age, or to any woman other than her close family. She does not even eat with other family members; instead, her food is taken in to her. She is only permitted outside her little hut briefly at night to perform her ablutions.

When the female Wayuu finally emerges there is a great celebration and she engages in special dance rituals to signify her availability as a young adult, ready for marriage. During the dance she must attempt to trip up the young males dancing with her, symbolically establishing herself in a dominant role. As she lives in a society controlled by women, and with all property passed down through the female line, she will already carry some authority in her new role, and it is her bridegroom-to-be and not she who must provide a dowry. This is the opposite of so many other cultures and the Wayuu themselves explain the long period of confinement for their young women as a time for learning so that they will become well-schooled in running tribal affairs when their time comes. They feel it is important that a young woman should not be faced with the burden of rearing a family until she has been fully educated in tribal crafts, legends and traditions.

The Female Curse

In many tribal societies, special ceremonies are performed in connection with menstruation. The first menstruation, when girls reach puberty, attracts particular attention. Even for primitive tribes it was clear that the arrival of menstrual bleeding was somehow connected with the potential for child-bearing. They believed that mysterious spirits entered the women's body. If the spirits were friendly they produced a good child. If they were hostile, they produced a bad child. In order to ensure that they were friendly, certain puberty rituals had to be carried out for girls who were experiencing their first menstruation. If these rituals were not observed and she gave birth, her child would be the incarnation of hostile spirits (a 'demon birth') and the tribe would put it to death. So observing the rituals of menarche became crucially important.

The female puberty rituals were many and nearly always unpleasant. They included such impositions as forced seclusion, fumigations, restricted diet, removal of pubic hair, wearing of a special apron, blood-letting, fasting, tattooing and mechanical defloration.

Each tribe had its own special version of these restrictions for menstruating girls, including the following, collected from a variety of sources: not being allowed to talk to men or boys; not eating from vessels used by other members of the tribe; having to cook their own food; not eating food that contained blood; having to eat alone; not being allowed to weep; not using perfumes; not playing games; not cleaning the mouth or teeth; not talking to another menstruating woman; not touching babies or small children; not looking in a mirror; not serving drinks or entering wine cellars; not lighting a fire; not mounting a horse or any other beast of burden; not travelling in any vehicle, not walking across a public road; having to sit crouching in a corner facing the wall; only being able to leave the house at night; walking about on blocks tied to their feet, and not touching children's toys.

ATTENTION

To maintain the religious purity
and cleanliness of this temple :
Women during menstruation
should not enter the temple.
Do not climb on or deface
temple structures.
Wear suitable clothes and
observe polite manners.

*Coming of age. A Wayuu girl in Colombia is
subjected to strict confinement on reaching
puberty (left). In some tribes, superstitions
about menstruation may demand the
removal of a woman to the edge of her
village, and isolation from all social contact
(above). Menstruating tourists visiting a
Balinese temple today may be surprised to
find themselves banned from entry (top).*

This is merely a sample of the restrictions that existed in various tribal societies, many of which are still in force to this day. The list is endless and the details vary from culture to culture, but they all have one thing in common: the menstruating woman is somehow dangerous. Her body is bleeding, not because she has injured herself but because she is possessed by evil spirits. As a result, she actively emanates evil. She is not merely dangerous to touch, she can also somehow give off an invisible, damaging substance. And her menstrual blood is itself toxic. It follows that (a) she must sleep apart; (b) she must not come near anyon; and (c) she must not touch anything of value. The simplest way to achieve all this was to shut her away completely during her period, often in a special hut (or even a small cage), but where such extreme measures were not taken she had to avoid a whole range of sensitive contacts that were considered important in each tribe.

She was especially dangerous at the time of her first menstruation, but it did not end there. With each subsequent menstruation, she would have to suffer some degree of restriction. Throughout their lives, women were always thought to be 'unclean' during their monthly periods and were faced with repeated taboos. Above all, they were required to refrain from sexual activity. If they did not do so, their husbands would suffer terribly. In some tribes it was thought that the man's sex organs would become diseased; in others, that he would lose his virility; in still others that he would be faced with ill-fortune in all his pursuits.

The ingenuity employed in devising more and more frightening punishments for husbands who co-habited with menstruating wives is amazing to behold. To give just one example: St Jerome is quoted by Thomas Aquinas as saying that a couple that makes love when the woman is menstruating will produce a baby that is 'deformed, blind, lame and leprous'. This terrible fate was not merely to remind them of the awful sin they had committed but also to demonstrate their monstrous behaviour to the rest of society.

All these cruel superstitions were gradually replaced as time passed. What had been dangerously evil became merely unclean and unaesthetic. As beliefs in possession by evil spirits faded, a concept of modesty prevailed and it was then considered merely impolite to be menstruating. Finally, it was looked upon as no more than unhygienic. In modern urban society, menstruating women may still talk about suffering from 'the curse', but they no longer take it seriously. They treat it as a minor medical inconvenience, rather like having a runny nose when suffering from a cold. However, despite this new enlightenment and the relegation of menstrual taboos to the fear-ridden tribal past, a few of the old superstitions do cling on, even today.

It comes as a shock to a Western tourist, for example, to find a notice in English outside a monkey temple in Bali, that states: 'For the sake of religious purity, menstruating women should not enter the temple precincts'. The fact that some of the female monkeys scampering about on the temple walls, freely urinating and defecating there, are probably also menstruating, is an irony that is lost on the religious authorities of Bali. What is important to them is that any *human* female entering the sacred precincts will somehow contaminate the holy place. Such is the stigma attached to this simple bodily function that its early mythology has somehow managed to survive the arrival of modern scientific knowledge.

Bali today is essentially Hindu, while the rest of Indonesia embraces Islam. Muslims, like Hindus, have a restrictive view of menstruation. In the Koran it is clearly stated that menstruation '…is an indisposition. Keep aloof from women during their menstrual periods and do not touch them until they are clean again.'

Like the Hindus and the Muslims, the Christians also viewed the menstruating woman with an irrational distaste. Some Christian countries have put this prejudice behind them, but others have not. In Greece, for example, the old taboos still survive. There, a menstruating woman is banned from entering a church or from taking communion, and she may not touch wine or bake bread. If she touches the wine it will go sour; if she touches the bread it will not rise.

In Spain similar restrictions are still applied in gypsy communities. A menstruating gypsy is not allowed to cook or to make love. The same is true in India, where Brahmin women, during their period of menstruation, must sit apart for four days. Nobody is supposed to touch them, but if they do so they must immediately have a bath to cleanse themselves. The only menstrual taboo we have left in the West now is the use of a blue liquid, instead of red, to represent menstrual blood in television advertisements for sanitary towels.

There is now a whole museum devoted to the subject of human menstruation. The Museum of Menstruation in Hyattsville, Maryland, which opened in August 1994, traces the roots of the taboos associated with it and analyses the ways in which so many societies have treated menstruating females as unclean by making them suffer social isolation and other restrictive ordeals.

What lies behind this horror of menstrual blood? Tribal people will have encountered plenty of blood in other contexts – from accidents and injuries, and the killing of prey. Blood from those sources did not create any special problems, so why menstrual blood?

The deeper answer, below the level of superstitions or conscious thinking, probably had to do with the biological significance of this type of blood. When a woman menstruates she is saying, in effect, 'I have failed to become pregnant'. In small, sparsely populated tribal societies this was a serious matter. For the tribespeople it was disastrous and shameful, but in a massively overpopulated, modern society it is more often a cause for celebration. For urban humanity there is no longer any disgrace attached to the condition of non-pregnancy.

Bearing this in mind it is extraordinary that in some societies, where urbanization has taken place and where there is also massive overpopulation – as in the case of India – there is still, even today, a prevailing attitude that sees menstruating women as unclean. This is a case of an ancient human superstition remaining on the shelves of society long after its sell-by date.

Perhaps this persistence of old customs reveals an additional, hidden factor in the significance of menstruation taboos, something beyond the question of pregnancy versus non-pregnancy. Perhaps it has as much to do with the denigrating of females by males as with the criticism of non-breeding. Male-dominated cultures will always welcome any female biological weakness that can be exploited to maintain male supremacy and perpetuate the unfair subjugation of women. Like the blood of birth, the blood of the menstrual flow is a useful weapon to use against women by cowardly male religious bigots.

There remains the biological question as to why women should have evolved such a liberal blood-flow during menstruation. Why not simply reabsorb the debris that appears in the uterus once a month? Other mammals may menstruate, but none does so in such a dramatic fashion. It looks suspiciously as though there may be some positive evolutionary advantage involved. Why would prehistoric woman, without the advantages of modern tampons, want to interfere with her active life in this strange way?

An ingenious answer to this question was put forward recently by anthropologist Chris Knight. He was intrigued by the fact that women living closely together tend to synchronize their menstrual cycles. (And it is said that, in the 1960s, whole populations of young girls had their cycles synchronized following pop concerts at which they all screamed together and became emotionally uninhibited en masse.) His theory suggests that, back in our hunting past, all the women of any particular tribe would have had synchronized cycles, simply because they were all living so close together. By evolving a more liberal blood flow they made themselves simultaneously unappealing to their men. This had the effect of going on strike sexually once a month, which, in turn, had the effect of spurring the men to go off on lengthy hunts until the bleeding was over, with the promise of sex when they returned with the kill. Hunting was always easiest during the full moon, so the cycle became a monthly one, and in this way ensured regular feasts at appropriate intervals.

The only drawback with this idea is that, in the primitive tribe of which he speaks, most of the adult women will have been pregnant or lactating most of the time. Nevertheless it is an intriguing theory and the only one so far to offer an explanation of the excessive blood-flow of the human female.

It cannot be denied that the 'curse' remains a nuisance even today. Apart from the necessity to stem the flow of blood, there is also the accompanying change of female temperament. This has been disputed by some feminists as yet another attempt by males to denigrate females, but that is unfair. There is statistical evidence that, during the period immediately leading up to the start of menstruation, there is a measurable degree of emotional disturbance, part of a condition known as premenstrual syndrome or PMS. For example, studies in hospitals have revealed that just over half the women admitted with injuries caused by driving accidents were at this phase of their menstrual cycle. This is over three times higher than might be expected if the monthly cycle was of no importance. Interestingly, interviews with some of the women drivers involved revealed that they felt unusually aggressive in the premenstrual phase and that it was this that led to the increased accident rate. This would fit well with the theory of prehistoric women spurring men on to leave for the hunt. By becoming irritable and uncooperative just before their blood-flow started, the changing mood of the women would have heralded the crucial monthly phase when, as one commentator put it, 'Men must hunt and women must bleed'.

Pair-Formation

With childhood behind them and the young male and the young female now both reproductively active, the moment has come for what will probably be their most impressive rite of passage between the dramas of being born and of dying – the moment of pair-formation. All over the world, in a hundred different ceremonies, young adult couples declare their profound attachment to one another in the presence of their friends and loved ones.

This type of public ritual has several functions. It demonstrates the status of those participating by involving lavish, almost wasteful expenditure; it persuades the other members of society to inconvenience themselves as participants in the ritual; it displays to all potential rivals the exclusivity of the new bond and it underlines the change in social standing of the new couple.

Wedding ceremonies vary considerably, but they all contain a characteristic sequence of symbolic acts that accompany the making of public vows. The true meanings of these symbolic acts are largely forgotten and they are now performed automatically, without question. The typical Western wedding, for example, is riddled with ancient superstitions designed to protect the young couple and ensure that their pair-bond is successful and fertile. Few people are aware of these.

The wearing of a veil by a bride, for example, should not be confused with the veiled state of Arab women. It was not intended to hide the bride's beauty, but rather to protect her from the evil eye. It was believed that, just before she was married, a bride would be at her most attractive to the Devil and that evil forces would be drawn to her overt display of innocence and virginity. To hold them back, a bridal canopy was introduced and this was eventually reduced to a mere facial covering. Once the service was over it was considered that, as a married women, she came under the powerful protection of her new husband, so the danger was past and the veil could be lifted.

The bride's white wedding dress is usually thought of as symbolizing virginity, but its origin was slightly different. It was a sign of high status because, by being so different from ordinary day dresses, it could never be worn again. In other words, it was a deliberate waste of money, worn to show that the bride could afford it and was therefore a valuable partner for her new husband. Less fortunate brides chose dresses of other colours that could be used again and again.

The requirement to wear 'something old, something new, something borrowed and something blue' had it origins in saying farewell to the bride's old life and celebrating her new one. Blue was said to be the colour of purity, and the borrowed item was meant to come from a married women who had been lucky in her marriage.

At early weddings the young men present used to fight one another for the bride's garter, which would bring them good luck. These tussles became so violent that they were later replaced with the bridesmaids fighting, in a genteel fashion, for the bride's bouquet, thrown backwards into the air. The flowers, being the sexual organs of plants, have a special meaning to the young women, who looked upon the capture of the bouquet as a symbol of finding a future mate.

Today the wedding speeches are often little more than a polite vote of thanks to the people involved, but that was not their original function. In antiquity they were made by jokers or jesters whose official duty was to be obscene. This was not done to shock the guests, but to divert the attention of the supernatural forces that would always gather at happy events. These obscenities, yet another form of protection against the evil eye, were also eventually banned. Today, if a wedding speech contains a few rude stories, many people imagine that this represents bad taste and is a modern decline in standards when, in reality, it is upholding a long and ancient tradition.

The wedding cake began as a fertility symbol. It was supposed to be broken up into small pieces and then handed to the groom, whose duty it was to throw it over the head of his bride. The more pieces it was broken into when it was thrown over her, the greater was the couple's chance of having many children. Originally, the wedding cake took the form of wheaten biscuits, the wheat symbolizing fertility. These biscuits later became wedding buns which were thrown over the bride by everyone present and then piled up as a centre-piece at the wedding feast. Later, the virginal white icing was added to the heap of buns by a French chef, and this led to the tiered wedding cake of today.

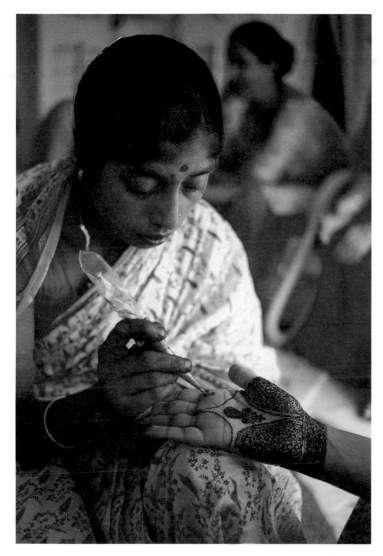

The garlanding of the groom at a Sikh wedding (far left). Marriage ceremonies remain the most elaborate and colourful of all the various passages of life.
The henna night (left): the bride-to-be is decorated with protective signs to defend her against evil spirits that may be attracted to her wedding festivities.

Instead of having the cake thrown over her, the bride now had to take a knife and cut it into slices to give to all present. The groom's hand guides hers, a remnant of the time when he heaped the cake over her head. The need for everyone to eat a small piece of wedding cake is to ensure that they too wish for children from the marriage. Anyone refusing a slice today (probably on the grounds of dieting) is, in old terms, performing an evil act that wishes the couple to be barren.

Today, because wedding cake is eaten rather than thrown, the guests replace the lost cake in the form of confetti. The word 'confetti' comes from 'confit', referring to sugared almonds. So the pieces of confetti are meant to be fragments of paper food. The old traditions die hard and usually manage to resurface in some way.

In each country the wedding ceremony has its own special, local rules. Although the central theme is the same, the details vary considerably. In a number of countries, from

North Africa through the Middle East to parts of Asia, there is a special skin decoration applied to the bride a few days before her wedding night. This takes the form of the application of an orange-red stain called 'henna', meticulously painted in delicate and elaborate patterns.

Henna cosmetics are made from the powdered leaves of a small shrub called Lawsonia. After a ritual bathing, the bride-to-be is dressed in her wedding finery and made to sit very still with her eyes shut while a female artist called a 'hennaria' paints the henna designs on her hands and feet. Once she has finished, she bandages the bride's hands and places them inside two embroidered bags to ensure that they dry without smudging. The feet may also be wrapped in pieces of linen. Usually the hands and feet stay bound up like this for a whole night. After they are exposed, the henna patterns will normally survive for about three to four weeks, after which they may be renewed. The night on which this decoration takes place, with the bride surrounded by her female friends, is referred to as 'the henna night', and it has been suggested that the British term 'hen night', which was first used in the 1880s, was borrowed from this.

What makes the henna ritual of special interest is the fact that the designs employed – which include such motifs as stars and crosses – are thought to protect the bride from evil spirits. Once again, there is the ancient superstitious belief that the serene happiness of the wedding ceremony will attract evil forces to the blissful couple and that they will therefore require an extra dose of protective magic. Covering the body in intricate, protective signs is seen as the best way of repelling the evil eye. Henna is said to possess a kind of 'virtue' which purifies the wearers from 'earthly taint' and renders them immune from the attacks of the devil and his agents. This is an amazingly common and widespread theme in many types of human ritual and it persists even in those cultures where superstitions are no longer taken seriously and where the true meaning of the actions is not understood.

These henna-decorated Arab weddings usually last for three days, but in some other cultures the ritual may be even more drawn-out. In a small Greek village, for example, the whole procedure may last for as long as a week. In the days before the wedding service the bride's dowry is carried through the streets and displayed in a special room. She and her female relatives will have been preparing decorated fabrics long before the great day arrives.

On the Thursday before the wedding all the female friends of the bride attend a special 'making the bed' ceremony, at which they throw money or other gifts onto a brand new bed as presents for the bride. They also throw flowers, sugared almonds and rice to encourage the fertility of the couple. The bed is then made, using new sheets, symbolizing virginity. In the old days they would have returned the day after the wedding night to examine the sheets for virginal blood and would then have displayed them to the village. Lastly, a baby boy is bounced on the bed to encourage the future birth of a son. Also, at the wedding itself, a toast will be drunk to the future son they hope to have.

On the wedding day, female relatives dress the bride in virginal white and sing to her, lamenting her departure from the bosom of her family. Male friends dress and shave the bridegroom, watched by his weeping mother, and there are laments and tears of sadness at the loss of the groom from his parents' home. The procession to the church is led by a man carrying a large cross. On the top and arms of this cross are placed ripe apples – again, a symbol of desired fertility. In yet another fertility ritual rice is thrown over the couple as they approach the church.

At the wedding service both bride and groom are adorned with white crowns and the groom reads out the epistle that declares that the woman is subject to the man. As part of the ceremony, the couple must circle slowly round the altar three times, while being pelted with rice and sugared almonds – more fertility magic. After they leave the church the couple dance in the village square along with all the villagers. The white crowns are later placed above a small altar, where they will remain to remind the couple that their bond of attachment is eternal. When they reach the door of their new home, they are greeted by a villager holding a saucer of rice. The couple scoop up handfuls of rice and then scatter this over the threshold. The bride then takes the saucer and smashes it, symbolizing the breaking of her maidenhead. Both bride and groom then drink honey, traditionally viewed as an aphrodisiac, to increase their chances of procreating.

In some countries, the dowry that has to be brought to the wedding by the bride can become a huge burden. In India this may lead to what has been described as the 'dowry murders'. In such cases, baby girls are killed by their families in order to avoid having to assemble expensive dowries for them when they have grown up. Here, as in many other parts of the world, marriages are arranged to suit the convenience of the two families involved. The young couple may never meet before their wedding day and must hope that their later intimacy breeds love as well as children. All too often it fails to do so, with unpleasant results, the wife remaining little more than a commodity to be casually disposed of, should the husband die.

In some arranged-marriage cultures the bride-to-be takes steps to protect herself, should anything go wrong with her married state. In the Yemen, for instance, she takes the remarkably sensible precaution of spending her dowry money on jewels and ornaments which she will then keep as her own personal property. They will act as an insurance policy for her – a wedding pension – if her marriage fails or if her husband dies.

The bringing of a dowry is essentially a demonstration of the inferiority of the one who gives it. The bride says to the groom, 'If you take me you can have all these gifts to compensate you'. It follows that, if a society is female-dominated, then the dowry should come from the groom, not the bride. This is precisely what happens in the Wayuu tribe in Colombia. There, inheritance is through the female alone, not the male, and it is the groom and his family who must bring gifts if he is to acquire a bride. Once again, the marriage is an arranged one, organized by senior relatives, and it is the bride's uncle who masterminds the acceptance of the gifts, usually consisting of beautiful gold ornaments and farm livestock. If these are found acceptable, only then can the bride and groom meet one another and become a new couple.

In each wedding ceremony the rite of passage is performed in such a way that the two sexes demonstrate their relationship in some kind of symbolic action. As the ceremony proceeds it is made abundantly clear who is dominant and who is subordinate. The fact that the female partner nearly always loses her family name and adopts her groom's name clearly supports an underlying bias in favour of male domination. In Estonia, this symbolic change is acted out in the form of a ritual in which the bride writes her maiden name on a piece of paper, places it in a bottle and then throws the bottle into the sea. From that moment on she will never use the name again. However, it has been pointed out that, although this act officially symbolizes the loss of the bride's family name, the reality is that it is still there, safely enclosed in the bottle that perhaps floats forever on the ocean currents. This could be taken to mean that it is never truly lost, but merely bottled up.

A more overt way of saying 'I wish to retain my identity and my equality' is to be found today in the more informal pair-formation ceremonies of North America. There the language of the service has been modified and the bride is no longer given away. In cultures where genuine sexual equality is slowly returning after thousands of years of male domination, one can expect to see a symbolic equality in the public ceremonies of betrothal to match the private equality of social life. Alternatively, one can expect to find an increasing number of young adult couples who simply ignore the rituals and start to live together, as a pair, but without any public formalization of the relationship. With the increasing decline of religious fervour, and the increase in female social standing, this is happening more and more. A report

The annual rowing regatta in Malta's Grand Harbour. At such sporting rituals groups of men reinforce their bonds of friendship.

on babies delivered in the UK in 1995 stated that, 'More than a third of babies delivered in England and Wales…33.9 per cent…were born out of wedlock'. Ten years earlier, in 1985, this figure had stood at only 19.2 per cent, so clearly there is a major trend under way as females assert themselves more and more vigorously.

The Return of the Gang

Because the new pair-bonded condition separates the young couple from their old social groups, they sometimes become too isolated from the community in which they live. During the early years of marriage this is not such a serious problem because they are focused on the major task of rearing children. But as the children grow up and the couple reach middle age there is a risk that a husband or a wife may suddenly feel 'too married', too inward-turning. For many couples, this feeling is counteracted by the arrival of a second wave of separate all-male and all-female activities. The schoolboy gangs and all-girl cliques of childhood, so strongly unisexual in character, reappear in a new, more sedate form as adult clubs. There are many different kinds of sporting or gambling clubs for men, such as *boules* in France, darts in England, or poker in America; there are dining clubs, social clubs and gentlemen's clubs, and pubs, bars and institutes. All these organizations beckon the wedded male and woo him back to the bosom of the all-male gang.

In the male-dominated Middle East the all-male groups of middle-aged men are a major feature of social life. In the Yemen, for example, every afternoon the men gather together in small groups where they spend several hours discussing the events of the day. They do this under the influence of a mild narcotic called *khat* (also spelled *qat* or *kat*), the use of which has become a national pastime, at least for males. It is estimated that 80 per cent of the adult male population indulges in this activity and it is claimed that little of the country's business is conducted without its aid. An economic report on the country commented, 'Land once used for export crops – cotton, fruit, and vegetables – has been turned over to growing a shrub called *qat*, whose leaves are chewed for their stimulant effects by Yemenis, and which has no export value.'

For these strictly all-male activities, the men gather in private rooms where they sit in a circle and start plucking the buds and fresh young leaves of *khat* from twigs cut from bushes of *Catha edulis*. These are thrust into the mouth until the cheeks are swollen with vegetable matter. Contemplative social chewing then begins until the narcotic effects start to take effect. Discussion then gets under way and chewing is resumed from time to time to release more of the chemicals into the mouth.

Khat contains drugs similar to amphetamine and ephedrine and it is said that it acts as 'an aid to thought and decision-making'. As a stimulant it is variously described as producing a feeling of exaltation, a feeling of being liberated from space and time, and of creating feelings of bliss, euphoria and clarity of thought. However, over-indulgence may lead to 'extreme loquacity, inane laughing and eventually semi-coma'.

These *khat* afternoons are far more than mere drug sessions. They have become woven into the cultural fabric of the country as the setting in which adult males become bonded into intimate social groupings. And they serve to maintain, on an almost daily basis, the deep split that exists between the world of the adult Yemeni male and the adult female.

In the United States this desire to return momentarily to the one-sex groups of childhood takes some strange forms. Some men participate in bizarre 'promise-keeping' ceremonies, while other groups take to the woods like overgrown boy scouts, banging drums and seeking what they refer to as 'inner male peace'. Some groups set off on hunting trips – where the male company is more important than the quarry – while yet others become embroiled in more warlike pursuits and play wargames with expensively adult toys.

Western females are generally less bellicose, expressing their non-marital side in activities more centred on caring rather than hunting or warring. They can more usually be found engaged in good works, looking after the sick, children or animals, sitting on charity committees or attending bridge clubs.

As mid-life mellows into old age, the difference between the sexes becomes less and less emphasized. With reproductive activity now a distant memory, the rites of passage that do occur usually involve males and females in much the same way. Even at the end of life, however, there are still a few distinctions to be made.

Life span

A well-known difference between the sexes is that women live longer than men. In the developed countries the average is about seven years longer for women. To be more precise, in Britain, New Zealand and Germany it is six years; in Canada, Australia and

Holland it is seven years; in the United States it is eight years and in France it is nine years. Even in the developing countries there is a two or three year difference in favour of the females. Everywhere women live just that little bit longer than men and it looks as though this is a basic biological feature of our species.

Nothing could symbolize this life-span difference between the sexes better than an extraordinary event that took place on 21 February 1996 in the town hall of the southern French city of Arles. There, Madame Jeanne Calment, the oldest person in the world – indeed, the oldest person who has ever lived in the entire history of our species – celebrated her 121st birthday.

She was born in Arles in 1875. Unlike other claimants to the title of the oldest person in the world she has accurate records to prove her title. And her life spans the whole history of our modern world. For instance, when she was one year old, Bell invented the telephone; when she was two, Edison built the first gramophone; when she was ten, the first petrol-driven vehicle appeared; when she was 13, the first film was shown; when she was 26, Marconi sent the first radio message; and when she was 28 the Wright Brothers took the first flight.

Her memory remains clear. Even today she recalls seeing the Eiffel tower being built when she paid a visit to Paris. And her sense of humour survives. When asked the secret of her long life she explained, 'I keep calm. That is why I am called Calment'. But perhaps her most astonishing memory is of an event that took place in Arles when she was a teenager serving in her father's shop, back in 1888. It was then that she sold paints to none other than Vincent Van Gogh, who was creating some of his greatest masterpieces in Arles at the time. She remembers him very well because he was as ugly as sin, evil tempered and smelled of booze.

Madame Calment was still riding a bicycle at the age of 100, and her heart has beaten four and a quarter thousand million times. But she has certainly not been a health fanatic. In fact, for those who find modern health regimes hard to follow, it must be reassuring to learn that she has always been a gourmet with a love of both alcohol and cigarettes, chocolates and sweets. Her favourite dishes are recorded as foie gras and a Provençal stew made with olive oil and garlic. At the age of 117 she was advised to give up drinking port and to stop smoking, but she was caught by a photographer happily puffing away at a

Sadly Madame Calment died in 1997, but even today remains the oldest person who ever lived.

cigarette when she was 118. To celebrate her 121st birthday she made her first record, a funk rap number called 'Mistress of Time'.

Madame Calment epitomizes the longevity of the human female. But why should women live longer than men? Is it, as suggested, truly a biological difference, or is it merely cultural? A glance at history

Madame Jeanne Calment of France, here celebrating her 121st birthday, is the oldest person who has ever lived.

suggests that it has been a variable phenomenon. In earlier centuries it would seem that, in some regions, men did indeed live longer than women. Skeletal evidence from prehistoric times tells us that men then lived about 20 per cent longer than women. In the Middle Ages, right up to the eighteenth or nineteenth centuries, European men were outliving women by seven or eight years. Then, at the start of the twentieth century, the position was reversed. Clearly there must be cultural factors at work, but are these the sole reason for life-span discrepancies between men and women, or is there an underlying biological difference?

The problem with historical comparisons between males and females is that their lifestyles change in different epochs. In earlier centuries more women died in childbirth, giving men the longer average life span. Today, under the intense pressures of urban business life, men are under more stress than women, who for their part, now have more advanced medical care. So the tables are turned and women live longer.

But does this mean that, in reality, there is no biological difference in longevity between man and women and that all the differences observed in the past have been due solely to varying cultural pressures? To find the answer it is necessary to seek out an environment where men and women enjoy identical lifestyles. This is not easy but it can be done. There is one location where gender is irrelevant and where both sexes follow precisely the same, relaxed, repetitive, ordered regime: inside monasteries and nunneries. In that cloistered world, where monks and nuns live under almost identical social conditions – no smoking, no drinking, no sex, no family problems, no business crises, no stress, same food, same fixed routines, same prayers – it is possible to analyse the records and find out which sex lives longer. When monastery and nunnery record books were studied and the life spans of 40,000 residents were examined it was discovered that, despite the similar lifestyles, there was still a significant difference in life expectancy between male and females. The nuns outlived the monks by approximately five years.

So there is, after all, a biological difference between the sexes in this respect. The evolutionary explanation would appear to be that grandmothers are more important than grandfathers. The significance of the grandparental role of older females has often been underestimated in recent years by our fragmented societies. But in ancient tribal communities, grandmothers must have been extremely important in helping their daughters with the heavy burden of maternal care. Of course, grandfathers also had a role to play, but the five extra years allotted to the elderly human female by evolution suggest that the elderly male was never quite as important as she was during later years of life.

Rituals of Death

Although females live longer than men, so that there are five elderly women for every elderly man, society no longer treats them in such a contrasting manner. But even at the end of life, the gender factor does not vanish entirely. Death has been described as the great leveller, but at the end of our lives there is the opportunity for human societies, for one last time, to signal their different attitudes towards males and females. Death may be genderless, but in some countries the rituals of death are certainly not.

For many centuries in India it was a Hindu custom for a widow to throw herself on her husband's funeral pyre, to be consumed in the flames along with his body. The official reason given for this form of female sacrifice – known as *suttee* – was that her husband would need her companionship in the next world and she dare not disappoint him. This was very much a one-sided ritual, however, there usually being no eagerness on the part of bereaved husbands to follow the same path.

Because it was outlawed by the British in 1829, an act of suttee has rarely been filmed, but reminders of it are everywhere. All over India, suttee stones commemorate the tragic events. The oldest known dates from AD 510.

Many women leapt voluntarily onto the fire at their husband's cremations, but others needed a great deal of persuasion. In some cases, pathetic widows were dragged screaming onto the funeral pyre by sons who were anxious about the cost of supporting elderly relatives. This provides a sobering commentary on the inhumanity of Hindu religious life and also on the unpleasant consequences of basing a society on loveless, arranged marriages.

The cruel practice of suttee can be seen as the ultimate expression of loyal monogamy or, perhaps more accurately, as a starkly sexist expression of wives as slave-like attendants of their lords and masters.

The abolition of suttee has not ended the misery of India's Hindu widows. In place of a quick fiery death, many now face a slow, living death. Callously spurned by their families

and shunned by society generally, they become social outcasts. Looked upon as witches, despised by everyone, forbidden to remarry, unable to find employment and condemned to beg endlessly for food, their existence is so terrible that they pray every day for death to claim them without further delay.

From all over India the sad widows flock to the holy city of Varanasi, where they hope to be purged by bathing in the sacred waters of the Ganges. Some of the estimated 16,000 widows in Varanasi today are as young as 11 years old, with decades of enforced mourning ahead of them. One bride, who was originally married at 10 and widowed at 19, has been waiting for death in Varanasi for 63 years and still it will not come. Observing the lives of these tragic women it is slightly easier to understand how new widows were once persuaded to perform the ancient custom of suttee.

Suttee is not the only example of gender roles resurfacing at funerals. In many other parts of the world, the ceremonies associated with death are used to ritually restate the inferior role of women in society. In Singapore, for example, at Malay Muslim funerals, only men are allowed to enter the cemetery. At other ceremonies women must keep apart from men and must wear different clothing. Societies where women are exploited or suppressed make use of almost every formal occasion to reinforce this, even where the rituals concerned are events as genderless as death.

In so many ways, society tries to underline the differences between the sexes by linking them to important, special events. Sometimes the differences have a biological basis, but often they do not. We seek to exaggerate the inborn qualities of maleness and femaleness as we try to intensify our personal identities. Nearly always we are using our gender as a flag to fly against the insecurities of life and the identity anxieties we feel as we pass through the often threatening human life cycle. In the process, we often subject ourselves to elaborate and unnecessary ordeals. Societies that breed self-confidence in their members need these displays less and less. As superstitions and secret fears recede into history, we will no doubt see a marked decrease in the artificial enlargement of the gulf between the human male and the human female.

Suttee – the Hindu female ritual of death, in which a wife threw herself on her husband's funeral pyre in order to provide him with a companion on his journey to the afterlife.

5

The Maternal Dilemma

The parental burden is greater for the human species than for any other animal on earth. It is this inescapable fact that lies at the heart of the maternal dilemma.

One of the greatest differences between the human male and the human female resides in the unequal distribution of parental duties. I am not referring to the vexed question of who gets up in the night to calm a crying baby, but to something so basic that we tend to take it for granted. I am referring to ownership of the womb.

To most people there is something inevitable about the idea of female pregnancy. To a zoologist there is nothing inevitable about it at all. Many animals reproduce with an entirely different system. For some, all the parental duties are carried out by the male, including the carrying of the developing embryos on their bodies. In those species, the female is fancy free, simply providing the eggs and then leaving the hard-working male to rear them on his own.

Mammals adopted a different strategy, with fertilization taking place not outside, but inside the female's body. There, snugly protected, the foetus was allowed to grow and develop until it was ready to be ejected into the outside world. Even then, after a long period of gestation, the female's unique role was not completed. Throughout the earliest part of her offspring's life outside the womb she had to allow it to continue to cannibalize her body, taking even more nourishment from her in the form of warm milk from highly modified sweat glands on her chest.

It may seem a bizarre thought, but there is no biological reason why, during copulation, the human female should not deposit her egg in the male penis, where it would burrow its way down into his reproductive system, make contact with his sperm, and then start to develop into a growing foetus. At the time of birth, the penis would enlarge into a temporary birth canal. After the birth, the male's chest would swell, not with pride, but with milk, and his nipples – nipples that he does indeed retain – would provide milk for the newborn.

I have only painted this strange picture as a reminder that, although many reproductive strategies are possible in the animal world, each species has evolved the system that is best suited to its own particular way of life. It is merely the accident of being born human that imposes the greater parental burden on our females but, unless they wish to remain childless, or adopt a child, it is an accident they cannot escape.

For many women there is no desire to escape. For them, bearing children is seen as the very essence of their existence, their most important achievement on earth. Everything else is secondary to that primeval activity. For others, there is a dilemma – the great maternal dilemma. They may have evolved an efficient womb and efficient breasts, but they have also evolved a high level of intelligence, a strong sense of ambition and an intense creativity. For some, living in today's already overcrowded world where breeding is no longer at a premium, exploiting these intellectual qualities is even more important than reproducing. They dislike the idea of becoming breeding machines and would hate to see their professional ambitions interrupted by a prolonged period of cumbersome maternal duties.

For the vast majority, however, there is a more ambitious desire. They want it all. They want to enjoy the full expression of both their wombs and their wisdom, but this is not an easy trick to pull off. Giving birth at the office is uncommon. Breast-feeding at a board meeting is a rare event. The woman who wants it all must develop a dual personality and somehow organize a double life. This is the burden that the human male does not face.

Birth

For the human female, the most dramatic experience in life is the moment of the first delivery. For countless thousands of years this act has been accompanied by comforting support from other females, the tradional midwives. Their presence has helped to calm the mother-to-be and to make her delivery quicker and less painful. This has always been – and still is – the practice for most tribal societies. Men were never allowed to be present at birth. There was a good reason for this. Most men are nervous when their wives are giving birth. Their anxiety transmits itself to the woman in labour and this slows down the birth process, making it more prolonged and more painful. The presence of close women friends and relatives, especially those who have already given birth themselves and who are therefore more calm as they assist, will help to relax the mother-to-be.

Without this calming influence, the woman giving birth will feel tense and fearful, and this condition sends signals to her brain telling her all is not well. This in turn makes the brain send out chemical messages saying 'there is a danger here, do not give birth yet'. This primeval protection device (against the presence of natural dangers) inhibits the delivery and, no matter how hard the mother strains and pushes, she will not be able to expel her baby. Only when she relaxes and feels more calm will an easy birth take place. In modern times we seem to have lost the knack of creating that sense of calm at the moment of birth and mothers the world over suffer for it. One only has to watch a film of a tribal mother squatting down on a few banana leaves and giving birth rapidly and then observe the prolonged agony of many a 'modern' birth to see the difference.

One feature of the modern birth is the fashionable idea of having the husband present to share the moment. This certainly gives him a stronger bond with his new baby, but if he transmits fear to his wife his presence is going to be damaging. His wife would be better off without him. If he is not displaying anxiety and is able genuinely to help calm his wife, then his presence will be invaluable. There are no hard and fast rules. Everything depends on the individual couple.

In tribal societies mothers and babies can stay close to one another. In urban societies this is not always so easy.

After the new baby has arrived there is a period of intensely active maternal care. In simple tribal societies this is a time when mother and baby are never apart. They are in intimate body contact almost the whole time. The baby is not put away from the mother. Even when she has returned to daily activities she will still keep it close to her and will travel with it slung on her body. The baby is programmed to expect this degree of contact and becomes distressed if it is separated from its mother. Babies hate being put away alone in a nursery and do their best to get back with their mothers by repeatedly giving alarm calls at night. Some of these cries are due to hunger, but most are simply demands for proximity. Sleepless nights for the mother can only be avoided when the baby has regained its natural place next to the parental bed.

The Urban Mother

In tribal communities the nature of the environment and the mother's activities do not clash with the demands of her new arrival. In the modern industrial world, this simple maternal harmony has all too often been lost. Mothers cannot cope. They cannot remain permanently close to their infants, like their primeval ancestors. The often miserable urban environment is totally unsuitable for children. In place of tribal affluence there is industrial hunger, dirt, poverty and redirected aggression. For millions of women today the dream of mothering has turned into a nightmare.

For some mothers the only way they can afford to feed their children is to leave them behind while they go out to work. The children need nourishment and maternal contact, but they cannot have both. Without food they will die, so the mothers have no choice. In

many developing countries, the working mother must endure tragic separations from her young ones. In the Philippines, for example, the international airport witnesses daily scenes of misery as mothers leave to work abroad in order to support their families. They can find good wages as maids and servants in other countries and are able to send money home to feed their infants in their absence. But to be good mothers in this way they must suffer separation from their loved ones, not for a few weeks or months but usually for several years. This is a totally unnatural maternal pattern, but they have little choice.

This is not a minor problem. The figures are startling. A recent survey revealed that no fewer than 2,750,000 Filipino women were working abroad. In addition to the maternal distress caused by the separation, educational authorities in the Philippines report that, 'Children of overseas workers often perform badly in school and grow up with little self-discipline because of the missing parent...Psychologically they are like orphans.'

Gender Bias

Another unnatural pressure modern mothers must face in some countries is a local gender bias. Where male babies are preferred over females, the sex ratio is brutally influenced by female infanticide. This is still widely practised in several regions of the world, even today.

Studies of smaller tribal communities over a long period of time have revealed that female infanticide increases during periods of severe food shortage. This has the long-term effect of increasing the ratio of hunting males to breeding females in the population. So, in these cases, it becomes a population control mechanism. This is not always the case. In larger communities it may have more to do with economic pressures. In India, for example, where poverty is widespread and where families are always expected to provide a large dowry when their daughters get married, giving birth to female babies can cause serious hardship. The so-called 'dowry murders' are the result, in which a female baby is secretly killed to relieve the family of the heavy burden of a dowry when she grows up.

Surveys of the sex ratio of adult humans in different countries give some surprising results. In Britain and America there are approximately 105 females for every 100 males. In India, reflecting the anti-female bias, the ratio is only 93 females to 100 males. In Pakistan the ratio is 92/100; in Bangladesh and Afghanistan it is 94/100. In China the ratio is even lower, with only 88 females to 100 males. It has been calculated that, altogether, these male-biased ratios add up to a total of something in the region of 60 million 'missing' women. It is not clear how many of these have disappeared as a result of infanticide, but it is difficult to see how else they can have vanished from the national statistics.

In China we do have some idea of how the ratio has been achieved. With a population of over one billion, the Chinese authorities made the laudable decision to reduce future increases. Their method in achieving this was, however, brutal and repulsive. All that is necessary to stabilize a population is to reduce the average family size for each couple to two children. In that way the offspring simply replace their parents. But in 1979 the Chinese leader Deng Xiaoping ordered the most extreme measures to be used. He was taken at his word and couples were officially permitted to have only one child. Most parents wanted a son and many baby girls were simply dumped on the streets.

Since 1979 over 15 million baby girls are said to have mysteriously disappeared in China. When a British television documentary was made, showing the infamous Chinese 'dying rooms' where baby girls are left to starve to death, the Chinese authorities hotly denied all accusations of cruelty. If we are to believe them, it remains to be explained what has happened to all the countless missing females in the present Chinese population.

In other countries there are also some strange statistics that are hard to explain. For example, it was recently discovered that in certain Arab countries in the Middle East there are only 484 females for every 1000 males. Again, it is not clear how this comes about, although from simple observation of these cultures it is obvious that boy babies are treated with much more care and attention than female babies. For example, boys are breast-fed for two years, girls for only one year.

Taken together, these instances of widespread gender bias with babies must add up to a mountain of misery for young mothers. After the months of waiting and the efforts of giving birth, every baby is precious in its mother's eyes. Or so it should be in simple biological terms. But it would seem that, in literally millions of cases, local culture then adds huge pressures to frustrate these natural maternal urges. How easy this is for the new mothers to accept we can only try to guess, but the likelihood is that in many, many cases there are long nights of agony and distress.

Mothers in other parts of the world, where this savage cultural interference with the biological process of human reproduction is absent, may not be faced with such acute,

Urban squalor creates a nightmare
environment for the human mother,
totally unsuitable for the rearing
of children.

heart-rending decisions, but they have their own special kinds of dilemma that they must face. In advanced cultures, where women wish to pursue serious careers and at the same time rear families of children, there are other kinds of conflicts and challenges. These can be solved either by involving other individuals to assist or replace the natural mothers, or by strategies involving these mothers themselves.

Maternal Solutions Not Involving the Mother

How can the modern woman solve her maternal dilemma? How can she be, at one and the same time, the primeval mother, fulfilled and enjoying the ancient satisfactions of maternity, while continuing to take an active part in modern social and business life?

One solution is to involve the father to a greater extent in the raising of the child. Today the working mother must interrupt her career to give birth and then to care for her baby during its earliest months. In some countries, however, the father is also given a chance. Paternity leave with full pay has become the latest step to give some degree of sexual equality to the parental couple.

In the United States the phenomenon of the house-husband has become increasingly common in recent years. When first proposed, at the height of the feminist rebellion, the concept of a housebound, pseudo-maternal male was viewed by most people as outlandish. The majority of men considered such an idea an affront to their masculine egos. However, as time passed more and more men found themselves in situations that demanded this solution to the maternal dilemma.

The typical scenario consists of wife and husband both working, with some of the money from their double income spent on professional carers for their small children. Then, without warning, the husband loses his job and finds himself sitting at home. The professional help is dispensed with as an economy and replaced by the husband himself. Because he has not chosen to become a house-husband but has had it forced upon him by the vagaries of the workplace, the role is less of an assault on his male ego than it would otherwise have been. The main attack on his self-esteem is the loss of his employment and the role of caring father provides more fulfilment than simply sitting around, idle and unemployed.

In this way, time and again, house-husbands were created out of necessity and this eventually led to the publication of a newsletter entitled *At-home Dad,* with the slogan 'Promoting the home-based father', as well as the formation of an organization called Dad-to-Dad with the stated goal of 'Bringing at-home dads together'.

Dad-to-Dad grew rapidly and could eventually boast branches in 11 states in the USA, as well as in Canada and Finland. The unconditional love given by fathers to their own children had a marked affect on the behaviour of the young ones. According to one report, they were less aggressive, more tolerant and less stressed than those left in day-care centres. The only problem was the negative social attitude towards the fathers concerned.

Although their numbers have now risen to two million in the United States alone, there is still a stigma attached to the lifestyle of house-husbands and some of them feel this so acutely that they pretend to be 'working from home' rather than admit that their activities are purely paternal. One of the main functions of the Dad-to-Dad organization is to provide moral support for such males and to ease the pain of social ridicule. They arrange 'Dad-Night-Out Dinners' at which men who might otherwise feel isolated and insecure can meet and exchange information. Despite facing derision, some individuals are now beginning to speak out about the deeply satisfying rewards of a full-time paternal role. The main benefit mentioned is their pleasure in the knowledge that their children are not being raised by strangers.

This greater involvement of the fathers in parental care can be immensely helpful to many working mothers, but it has to be admitted that the human male is less well adapted to parental care than his mate. His most obvious failing is that he cannot breast-feed the baby. All experts now agree that breast milk is far better than bottle milk for the growing baby. There are two separate reasons for this. First, the chemical constitution of the mother's milk is superior to anything that can be offered in a bottle, no matter how advanced the formula. Second, the actual process of delivering the milk to the baby is far more intimate and loving when it comes from the breast. This second point applies as much to the parent as to the baby itself.

An attempt to give to the caring father the same sensation of intense intimacy that the mother feels when breast-feeding has led to the invention of what is called a 'baby-bonder'. This Californian invention consists of two breast-shaped milk bottles that can be slipped over the head like a life jacket and worn as a 'breast bib' on the father's chest. They

The American 'baby-bonder' –
a specially designed pair of milk
bottles worn by the father to
simulate breast-feeding.

mimic the shape of the mother's chest and provide milk from two nipple-like teats. This means that the baby is held close and cuddled during feeding just as it would be if it were being breast-fed.

For the father who is secure enough in his masculinity to use one, this baby-bonder can, in theory, go a long way towards strengthening the father/baby emotional attachment. But it remains to be seen just how well the fathers concerned can make the imaginative leap into temporary motherhood, or whether they will feel pangs of embarrassment so strong that these will unconsciously destroy the sensations of true intimacy.

In many cultures the parental burden is lightened by the introduction of child-care specialists. This takes different forms in different parts of the world. In general, the nursery 'crèche' that replaces the mother can free her for other activities for many hours a week. But there are two prices to pay for this. First, prolonged periods of bonding between mother and infant are lost. Second, the way the infants are treated by the professional carers is bound to be different from that offered by the real parents. For example, the tiny children are liable to be taught male and female traditions that artificially widen the gap between the sexes. Or they may be indoctrinated with superstitious beliefs that lodge all too permanently in their receptive young brains. The parents have little or no control over the hour-by-hour experiences of these children, or of what they might be learning. They must trust in the carers and hope that the days their children spend with them will be comparatively trauma-free.

Although there are undoubtedly excellent child-care centres all over the globe, recent research has claimed that, with the best will in the world, problems may arise. According to an Italian research team from Milan University, infants who attend day nurseries from the age of one to three years and for more than seven hours a day, 'are more likely to have behavioural problems than those raised at home'. They are at risk of becoming bullies, showing less self-control and less respect for the rights of other children.

If this is true, it suggests that tiny children, left in the company of many others, are driven to toughen up their responses. Just as an older child can become 'streetwise' if exposed to a competitive urban environment, so a toddler can become 'crèchewise' if exposed to daily competition in the absence of its protective, watchful mother.

Despite this risk, it has to be said that day nurseries and crèches provide invaluable assistance to harassed working mothers who, although they might much prefer to look after their own children at home, have no choice in the matter. The crèche may not be perfect but, as one working mother said plaintively, it is far better for her little son to go to a day nursery 'than to sit at home watching the washing machine go round'.

Another, totally different solution has been suggested by an American lawyer. She lives a busy professional life, but when she goes home to her children she can be certain that they will have been well looked after in her absence, for a special reason. She is a member of a Mormon family and has eight co-wives. Whenever she is busy working she knows that there will be several of these co-wives at home taking care of all the children in the family. Because she knows them all so intimately, she can be sure that their relationship with her children will be as she would wish.

This successful lawyer has seriously proposed her polygynous state as the best of all solutions to the maternal dilemma, commenting, 'Women in monogamous relationships don't have this luxury. As I see it, if this lifestyle didn't already exist, it would have to be invented to accommodate career women.' Her point is that, in any group of nine wives, there will always be some who prefer to stay home and mind the babies and some who prefer to go out in search of challenging careers. A division of labour, not just between the sexes but also between the co-wives clearly works well for her, but could this arrangement become a major pattern of behaviour in Western society in the future? Some observers agree with her and query why there should be any legal or religious opposition to such an arrangement. The main objections, as discussed in Chapter 3, are that there will always be a risk of jealousies and rivalries between co-wives and, if the pattern became widespread, there would be the additional problem of what to do with all the frustrated, surplus males. Nevertheless, in exceptional cases where the ground rules have been established from the very beginning of the relationships, it is a solution to the maternal problem that may work well enough.

Keeping the problem in the family in a different and more traditional way, there is the grandparental solution. Using grannies to care for the children is genetically sound and as reliable as senility will allow. The long lives of adult females mean that they have many years of loving and caring to offer their descendants, if they are given half the chance. The average age for the menopause in the Western world is 51; the average life expectancy is 76. So there is a quarter of a century of non-breeding years left for the typical Western woman in the latter part of her life. This is a huge gap, during which time she remains, in most cases, full of caring, loving feelings. In communities where the old traditions have survived and the extended family has not been broken up and scattered, the grandmother solution remains an important answer to the maternal dilemma. Unfortunately, in many countries, the large extended families of yesterday are becoming more and more uncommon. Family mobility often destroys these bigger groupings and grannies are then too far away to be of casual day-to-day help.

A drastic measure is forced upon many mothers with large families, no husband, no money and no alternative but to go out to work simply to survive. It is the 'Little Mother' solution. When the family grows large enough, the oldest daughters are co-opted to act as mothers to the babies. At a time when most little girls would be playing with their dolls, these tiny girls are already weighed down with full parental tasks and responsibilities. Perhaps this function actually explains the obsession that small girls do have with dolls. Perhaps the love of dolls is not, as is usually supposed, a playful rehearsal for adulthood, but instead an acting out of the age-old role of the Little Mother when times are hard.

This view is supported by recent tests in which it was proved that, when boys and girls are given the choice of a wide variety of toys without any adult pressures on them to make particular choices, there is still a massive difference between the sexes regarding the preference for dolls. Time and again little girls unerringly gravitate towards these toys. This happens, apparently, even when they are encouraged to select politically correct 'non-sexist' alternatives.

The Fine-Tuning of the Mother

An objection has been raised to all these non-maternal solutions to the maternal dilemma. It is argued that, since mothers have been fine-tuned by evolution to care for their own offspring, other carers will never be able to match what the maternal figures themselves have to offer their babies.

There are many ways in which mother and baby bond together, some obvious and some not. For example, most mothers intuitively hold their babies in a certain way, with the little one's ear pressed close to the left breast. Like this, the infant is in the best position to hear the mother's heartbeat, a sound which has a dramatically calming effect on any baby. When infants in a nursery were played a recording of the sound of a mother's heart beating, they fell asleep twice as quickly.

There is an additional way in which the left-side holding of the baby may be of special benefit to it. New studies at the Hammersmith Hospital in London suggest that, while the baby's right ear is pressed to its mother's chest, listening to her heartbeat, its other ear may be particularly sensitive to her melodic, crooning voice. It is this *left* ear that feeds information to the *right*-hand side of the baby's brain, the half that is concerned with the processing of musical tones, melody and the emotional quality of sounds. All over the world young mothers intuitively coo, hum and sing lullabies to their little ones, using few words, but all employing the same kind of soft, gentle, tones. The left-side holding of the babies means that they will be better able to appreciate these loving sounds and this will,

The 'Little Mother' Solution. When a woman has a large number of children her older daughters can provide a valuable maternal-support system by helping to look after her new babies.

in turn, help to strengthen the bond of affection that is growing between mother and infant.

This is just one of the many ways in which mothers automatically know how to be close and intimate with their babies. Another maternal specialization concerns the sense of smell. It has been claimed that mother and baby can identify one another by detecting personal fragrance and that this is one of the ways in which the bond of attachment between them is strengthened. To confirm this, a simple experiment was devised to test the ability of young mothers. Could they really identify the fragrance of their own child and distinguish it from all others? Most mothers are not even aware that they are supposed to possess this ability.

A group of mothers with their babies was assembled in a garden. The babies were then carried away by nurses and cared for in a nearby house. The young mothers were then asked to stand in a row and were blindfolded. One baby at a time was then brought out into the garden and carried along the row by one of the nurses. Each mother was allowed a brief sniff as the baby went past her. When it had been carried down the whole row, its mother was asked to raise her hand if she had been able to identify it.

To their astonishment, the young mothers were correct almost every time. They had no idea they possessed this particular skill. In fact, the only mother to make a mistake was one who was so worried that she would miss her own baby that, in her anxiety, she identified someone else's as her own. Later, when her own child was passed in front of her she did, indeed, identify it correctly. When the fathers of the babies were tested in the same way, the success rate fell to about 50 per cent. So, although they had some skill in this direction, it was their wives who were truly outstanding.

Other tests have shown this fine-tuning works both ways. Not only can mothers identify their babies simply by their fragrance, but babies can identify their own mothers in a similar manner. If there is this kind of sensitivity in the maternal context, then it obviously follows that the best partnership, where babies are concerned, is with their own mothers rather than with some kind of substitute, no matter how loving the stand-in may be.

If improved fragrance-detection is an advantage to the human mother, it might be predicted that, as a result, women would have a better sense of smell than men. And this is indeed the case. When the two sexes are tested with a variety of odours, women nearly always out-score men.

(The domination of the wine trade by men is a case of ancient tradition overpowering modern knowledge. Perhaps because men secretly knew that women were better at this task, they created ridiculous superstitions to prevent any shift of power. One of these was the belief that if any woman so much as set foot in the wine cellar of a great vineyard, she would sour all the wine – said to be especially true if she was menstruating. It is hard to believe, but there are still some major vineyards in France where, even today, the presence of women in the cellars is strictly forbidden. At a few vineyards, however, modern thinking has prevailed and women have not only intruded, but they have taken over. When this happens they are scathing about the abilities of the male nose. One expert has commented: 'women have a more accurate palate…if a man recognizes the scent of white flowers in a wine, a woman will be able to say if the flower is eglantine or hawthorn.')

As part of the fine-tuning process, women also have better hearing. Mothers are able to identify their own babies simply by hearing them crying and, what is more, they can do this even in their sleep. Today, when we all live in separate houses, this is not so significant, but in ancient tribal settlements where there were many babies and mothers in earshot of one another, it was vitally important that every mother did not wake up every time one of the babies started crying for food in the night. During the course of evolution, the human mother became equipped with this special ability to wake up only when it was her own child that needed her, and this ability has remained with every woman to this day.

A poignant proof of the importance of a physically close relationship between a mother and her baby has emerged recently from some studies made at the famous Kaiser Permanente Hospital in San Francisco. There they have been encouraging what they call 'kangaroo care' in the case of premature babies, and it is working wonders. In the past, babies born prematurely have traditionally been isolated in transparent incubators and carefully monitored for vital functions. Lying there forlornly, with wires attached to their bodies, the minute infants, only a few pounds in weight, were left to grow and become slowly stronger until they were eventually considered hardy enough to be given to their mothers to hold.

This method has now been drastically modified. What happened was that doctors in a

South American hospital – where there was shortage of incubators – were forced to allow some mothers of premature infants to hold their little ones close to them, on the front of their bodies, like tiny kangaroo babies. To their surprise, the babies treated in this way put on weight much faster and were able to leave the hospital twice as early as the supposedly favoured ones that had been inside the incubators.

When this was discovered, doctors at the Kaiser Hospital decided to risk a similar procedure, not because they lacked incubators but to see if they could improve the growth rate of the premature babies. Mothers were encouraged to take their little ones out

As part of their maternal fine-tuning, women have a better sense of smell than men. Despite this, the wine trade is still dominated by men (above). 'Kangaroo care' of premature babies. If these babies are allowed daily contact with their mothers they develop much faster (right).

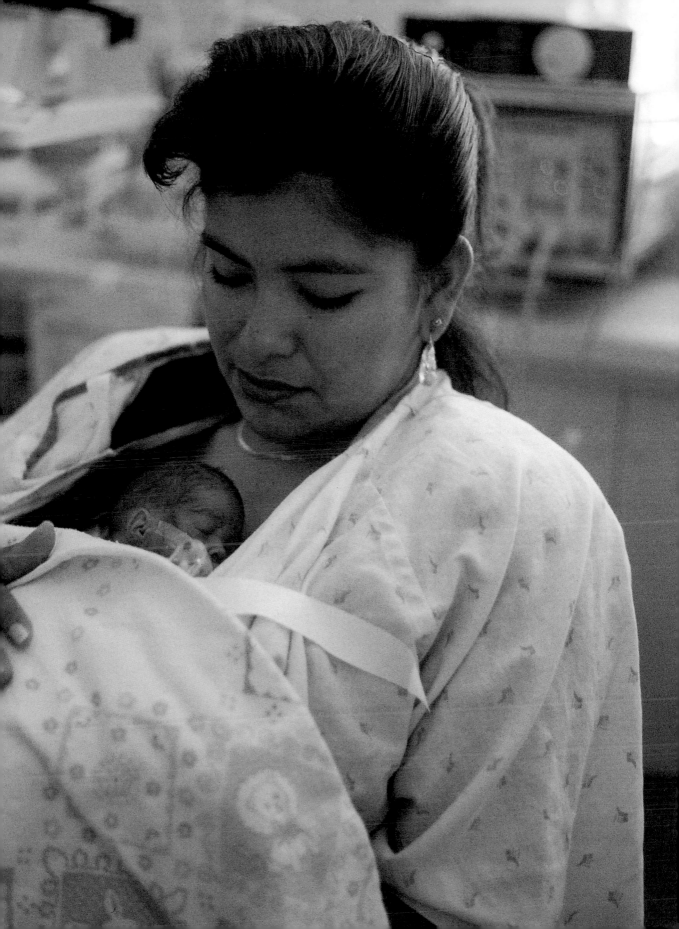

of their incubators for several hours a day and hold them gently on their chests. The babies in question are little bigger than newborn kittens and it is an astonishing sight to see these tiny objects sleeping contentedly on their equally contented mothers. The strain of incubator separation, for both of them, was gone. And, sure enough, they grew much faster and were able to go home twice as quickly. Nothing could provide more vivid support for the idea of special fine-tuning between the human mother and her baby.

Maternal Solutions

Because mothers and babies are so closely fine-tuned to one another, it follows that the very best of all the solutions to the maternal dilemma is one that involves the mother herself in some way. One such arrangement sees the mother continuing to do her job, but taking her baby with her to her place of work. This is the *Spatial Solution* and it is the one most favoured by tribal people or those engaged in primitive agriculture. In earlier days women labouring in the fields would attach their babies to swaddling boards and hang these up in nearby trees, like clusters of strange fruits. The tight swaddling gave the babies a sense of security, as if they were being snugly embraced, and hanging them up above the ground kept them safe. From the fields the mothers could see them clearly and could keep an ear open for any sounds of hunger or distress.

This solution is less applicable in a modern setting. The nature of modern labour and its location means that it is hard for a working woman to keep as eye on her baby as she toils away. In the hives of industry and the corridors of business power, it is difficult to be an attentive mother and an ambitious executive at one and the same time. An offspring in the office seems slightly out of place, as does a cradle in a conference hall. The only modern woman who can happily employ the Spatial Solution is one who normally works at home, but such careers are limited (although there are signs of change, thanks to the arrival of the home computer).

The most obvious alternative to the Spatial Solution is the *Housewife Solution*. Until recently this was considered the norm in Western society. If a young mother continued to work after giving birth it was frowned upon as inappropriate and improper. The young woman who wanted to start a family simply gave up all idea of doing anything else and concentrated exclusively on rearing her children. With a large family this could more than fill her day and, providing she was not overly ambitious or unduly poor, she could enjoy a fulfilling maternal existence.

In the modern world, however, with greatly improved education, women have rediscovered that, all along, despite male propaganda, they had excellent brains capable of competing with males in many fields of endeavour. This has led some to go to the other extreme and to sacrifice family rather than career.

The *Non-Breeding Solution* suits some women, individuals who are fired by ambition and who cannot flourish without a major career challenge. Many such women are now refusing to become chained to domestic chores and boldly reject the stigma attached to earlier expressions such as 'spinster' or 'old maid'. Today this rejection is much more easily accepted by society and such women, if they can avoid a lonely old age, can enjoy a rich existence. Liberated from family ties, their achievements have been impressive in many fields. If they wish to enjoy an active sex life, they can now rely on modern contraception or abortion to maintain their unencumbered position.

For some career-minded women, contraception is not enough. They opt for the more drastic strategy of early sterilization. Family planning clinics have recently been astonished to find girls as young as 18 arriving at their doors demanding permanent sterilization that will leave them free to pursue their careers single-mindedly for the rest of their lives, enjoying sex whenever they feel like it but avoiding all parental ties. Even the most ardent family planners find this worrying, knowing that future love affairs may lead to late maternal feelings and deep remorse. (It is said that 10 per cent of sterilized women live to regret their decision.) But despite such warnings, the figures for female sterilization are on the increase. A British professor of obstetrics, commenting in 1995, noted that five per cent of British women under the age of 30 have been sterilized. As one observer put it, 'The patter of tiny feet is losing its allure'.

In the past, medical records show that about 10 per cent of women have always remained childless for various unavoidable reasons. Recently that figure has doubled, the additional 10 per cent being voluntary non-breeders, either by means of sterilization, contraception, abortion, celibacy, or by finding sexual fulfilment through solitary sex or lesbian liaisons. With career opportunities increasingly free of gender bias in the West, it is highly likely that this trend will continue and grow stronger, but it may, in its wake, leave a

The Spatial Solution. In tribal and agricultural societies it is comparatively easy for the mother to remain close to her baby (above), but in the modern business world of urban society this is not always so simple (right).

large number of middle-aged women looking back on their youth and wistfully wondering whether perhaps their productive years should have been their reproductive years.

Considering the problems of the Spatial Solution, the Housewife Solution and the Non-Breeding Solution, it is clear that none of these maternal strategies is perfect in today's world. Each has its own special drawbacks. Mothers need to devote themselves to their babies and intelligent women need to express themselves. So what can be done? The answer is to be found in the longer life span of modern women and in their ability to control the size of their families. It is the *Temporal Solution*. There are two versions: breed young, rear, say, two children, and then devote the rest of your life to a career, or devote yourself single-mindedly to a career when young and then breed late, just before it starts to become dangerous.

With the first of these alternatives, the female breeds as young as possible – in her late teens or early 20s – sees her children through the sensitive years, and then embarks on a major career in her 30s. This is biologically more appropriate, because her body will be better suited to breeding at the younger age, but unfortunately modern educational systems are not ideally geared to what is rather insultingly referred to as the 'mature student'. Another disadvantage is that the brain is much better at absorbing masses of new information during the younger years and female students starting out on higher education at, say, 30, will find it more of a struggle than their 18-year-old companions.

Late breeding does seem to be the better option. Athletes and dancers are more or less forced to adopt this plan because, whether they like it or not, their careers go into a decline when they reach their 30s. So a successful athlete, sportswoman, ballet dancer or fashion model can try to cram a life's career into, say, 10 years, from age 20 to 30, and then have children in her early 30s. With luck she will then enjoy the double fulfilment that this strategy offers.

The late breeder can, of course, push maternity back a little further if she is prepared to take a risk. But in such cases it is important to know the dangers. Female fertility starts to drop after she passes the 30-year mark. It may drop as much as 50 per cent between the ages of 30 and 35 and continues to decline until the menopause is reached (the average age for which is 51). Also, it is important to remember that the risk of having a Down's Syndrome baby is eight times greater at 40 than at 30. By the age of 45 it is 27 times greater. Another disadvantage is that the sperm of men whose mothers were over 40 when they were born are less vigorous than those of sons of younger mothers. Despite these risks, the *Late Breeding Solution* is definitely on the increase. In Britain, for example, births among women aged over 40 have risen by 50 per cent during the past decade. (It has been suggested that this may account, in part at least, for the falling sperm-count in British males in recent years.)

For many modern women the modern maternal dilemma will never be solved. The urban environment makes it incredibly difficult. As a result, there will always be a risk of frustration and conflict within the family unit. The unfair way in which urbanization has treated the human female has certainly made its own special contribution to the ongoing battle of the sexes. Instead of the tender intimacies we should expect to find inside a close family relationship, what we all too often encounter is a competitive battle of wills, and these gender wars are the subject of the next and final chapter.

The Gender Wars

For a million years our ancestors played the courting game. As time passed, the game became more intense, more extended, more complicated. Brief sexual interludes gradually evolved into prolonged erotic intimacies. The hairy apes had sex; the naked humans made love. And, in the process, powerful bonds of attachment developed between males and females. That is to say, between particular males and particular females. The human pair-bond was born. In the simple tribal setting all was well and our ancestors flourished, spreading out across the globe to conquer the entire planet. But in their rush to global dominance, something changed, striking a note of discord between the males and the females. How did human sexuality survive the arrival of the modern urban condition? What happened to bring about the battle of the sexes?

We live in a time of great cities, where half the world's human population is caged in an urban zoo. Conditions there are unkind to simple loving family relationships. The great city may be full of novel excitements and ambitious possibilities, but it is a harsh environment for all those who fail to make it to the top. For the vast majority, all too often, there is stress and frustration. How can this pent-up emotion find an outlet?

The answer, sadly, is that the most convenient victim, the one closest to hand (or fist), is the sexual partner. The people who should be the most loved become the most abused, simply because they are there. In 1996 in the United States, more than two million cases of battered women were reported to the police – and many more went unreported. Because men are physically stronger than women, abused husbands are less common, although many will suffer a verbal battering when the pressures of the day become too much for their hard-pressed mates. Based on these USA figures, the following information emerges:

1. *Physical battering by a man is the single biggest cause of injury to women.* Even when all the injuries caused by road accidents, muggings and rapes were added together, the total obtained still did not exceed the figure for domestic violence. These figures suggest that as many as one in three women will be assaulted by their male partner at least once in their lifetime.

2. *When one partner attacks another, it is 10 times more likely to be the man that attacks the woman.*

3. *When pregnant, women are twice as likely to be battered by their male partners.* It is significant that, at the very time when women need the greatest protection and caring from their men, they receive instead the highest level of physical abuse.

4. *Long-term revenge is a key factor in human aggression.* Of the men who did the battering, 73 per cent were themselves battered as children. Redirected aggression is another key element in human violence. If we are not strong enough to attack our attackers, we turn elsewhere: 50 per cent of battered women beat their children. And it is a sobering thought that more than three million children witness acts of domestic violence each year. (It is does not come as much of a surprise to discover that at least 80 per cent of men in prison in the USA in 1996 grew up in homes where domestic violence occurred.)

5. *Of all the female murder victims, 30 per cent die at the hands of their male partners.* By contrast, only 4 per cent of male victims were killed by their female partners. (Intriguingly, the average prison sentence for men who kill their female partners is only two to six years, while for women who kill their male partners it is 15 years. If these figures are accurate, it means that the United States is still falling seriously short of true sexual equality.)

6. *Of the homeless women and children in the United States, 50 per cent are refugees from domestic violence.* Twenty years ago the first battered women's shelter was opened. Today there are 1500 of these shelters.

Because marital discord is so common today, we have sometimes wrongly imagined that this is an inevitable condition and that the battle of the sexes has raged throughout human history. Cartoonists often reflect this attitude by depicting our primeval ancestors as sexual brutes, the prehistoric caveman dragging his screaming mate off to their den by her hair. The truth must have been rather different.

Contrary to popular belief, our primeval days must have been amazingly affluent. We had discovered meat as a new and highly nutritious form of food and we had outclassed our carnivore rivals by inventing simple weapons. With group co-operation and language we rapidly became the most successful species on the planet, and before long we had occupied almost every corner of the earth. We could not have done this if our little tribes had been constantly squabbling, bickering and fighting.

Today we can get a glimpse of what life in a small tribe must have been like by watching what happens in one of the few groups of people that still live the same kind of lifestyle. A study of the Baka pygmies of West Africa, who remain hunter-gatherers to this day, shows us a culture in which men and women form lasting pair-bonds and enjoy the kind of harmony that has become increasingly threatened in the more 'advanced' urban societies. The concept of the 'noble savage' is often sneered at, but the concept of a peaceful tribe is far from being a fantasy. It is the caveman thug who is more likely to be the far-fetched fiction.

A key feature of early tribal life is that the men were away hunting for a great deal of the time, while the women remained at the centre of society in the tribal settlement. By combining the efforts of the men and the women, the whole tribe could feast together. The men relied on the women for many things – for gathering valuable vegetable food, for organizing the village, for building the little huts and preparing the feasts. The women relied on the men for animal food and for protection against outside dangers. It was a well-balanced system in which the sexes depended heavily upon one another.

The Mother Goddess

When primitive farming began, the breeding of animals and plants became a new way of life. The earth gave up her bounty and the early farmers began to see her as a gigantic mother giving birth to all the foodstuff that was to fill their horn of plenty. The mother earth then became personified as the earth mother, a huge, all-powerful female, a gigantic goddess whose fat-laden body symbolized the fat of the land.

All over the ancient world, representations of the Mother Goddess are found, always fat and always faceless. They were not individuals, they were emblems; emblems of fecundity and fertility. Most of the surviving figures of these early goddesses are small. They were easily portable and were probably carried in the clothing as a protection against possible misfortunes. Although early farming offered, for the first time, the huge bonus of a food surplus and food storage, it was at the same time highly vulnerable to sudden climatic changes such as floods and drought. The fertility of the land was a source of much anxiety, and the fertility of the goddess, therefore, was a major preoccupation. It followed that she had to possess female reproductive qualities in abundance. Frequently, this was represented by images that emphasized her reproductive organs – her breasts, her belly, her wide hips and her genitals. Sometimes these were the only details shown.

In addition to the small figurines there must have been huge effigies of her in early settlements, although few of these remain today. One of the most dramatic is to be seen on the small island of Malta in the Mediterranean. There, at the prehistoric temple of Tarxien, stands the lower half of a vast Mother Goddess. Originally, she must have stood at least 2 m (around 6 ft 6 in) tall, but the top half has been vandalized, probably destroyed by some pious knight who was offended by the idea that a woman could become such an all-powerful symbol of natural wealth. Even though today the statue is only fragmentary, it still serves to give us a clear picture of the might of the 'Great Mother'.

The Mother Goddess had two major roles to play: she symbolized the fertility of the crops and the domestic animals, and she also symbolized the fertility of the human female. In those early days the whole population of the world was extremely limited and breeding large families was vitally important. Women would pray to the Great Mother to make them fertile, to provide more children to work the land.

Many of the earliest effigies of the goddess are in the posture of giving birth. These were worn as amulets around the necks of women to aid them in becoming pregnant. This custom persists, even today, in remote parts of the world where the population is still small and women are still desperate to produce more and more babies. And the habit of carrying small fertility figures in their clothing is still in evidence. In some East African tribes, the women carry a small, highly stylized fertility figurine made from three spherical nuts, joined together to create a figure that is essentially a head with two breasts and no body. They believe that if they do not carry such an object they will run the risk of becoming barren. (In our overcrowded cities a more appropriate amulet today would perhaps be in the shape of a condom or a contraceptive pill.)

The Mother Goddess, the all-controlling maternal deity, dominated human society for thousands of years. She was seen as the source of all life and the nourisher of every living being. Her great body gave birth to everything that breathed and moved on the face of the

The primeval harmony of human family life, before the gender wars had begun, can still be seen in surviving tribal societies.

earth. Males were mere accessories – almost disposable – while she was the essential figure around which everything evolved.

Some have even suggested that, at this stage in the human story, the male's contribution to breeding was not understood. They argue that if copulation was not connected with birth in the minds of these early people, then the male's sperm would not have been seen as a significant part of fertility. The concept of the mother giving birth would therefore have been the only reproductive theme and this would explain the dominance of the Mother Goddess.

Although sexual ignorance provides an appealing interpretation of the dominance of

The largest of al the surviving mother goddess figures from ancient times, at the Maltese megalithic temple of Tarxien (3000 BC) (left). When complete she must have been over six feet tall.

A recently discovered Maltese mother goddess figurine (3000 BC) (below left).

A modern fertility figurine worn by African women to encourage pregnancy (below right).

the female deity, the facts do not support this explanation. Sexual knowledge must have been commonplace from the beginning of the agricultural revolution 10,000 years ago, since by then the true meaning of copulation had become widely understood as part of primitive animal husbandry. Without this knowledge the selective breeding of livestock would have been impossible.

In fact, the oldest writings known to man include phrases that leave nothing to the imagination. In a Paradise Myth from ancient Sumer, dating back to at least the third millennium BC (and written down about 4000 years ago), there is this passage: 'He embraced her, he kissed her, Enki poured the semen into the womb, She took the semen into the womb, the semen of Enki, One day being her one month, Nine days being her nine months, the months of womanhood'. Clearly, the 'facts of life' were well understood by this time. Because the god Enki was mating with a goddess, her divine pregnancy is accelerated from a mundane nine months to a mere nine days. But the fact that the ordinary pregnancy of 'womanhood' is known to be nine months demonstrates without question the ancient knowledge of the male role in reproduction.

Furthermore, as mentioned in Chapter Two, gigantic sculptures of the human phallus are known from the earliest days, indicating that the male's sexual significance was far from overlooked. Even so, for those who were reaping the rewards of early agriculture, the act of giving birth by the female would have remained the most vivid symbol of reproductive plenty.

As the ancient civilizations slowly grew in power and complexity, so the power of the Mother Goddess waned. One of her last representations was in the form of Diana of Ephesus, a sacred figure who flourished as recently as the first millennium BC. A colossal temple was built in her honour on the west coast of what is now modern Turkey. It was so vast (125 x 65 m, or 413 x 214 ft) that it took 120 years to build and became one of the Seven Wonders of the ancient world. Today, when we marvel at the mighty Parthenon in Athens, it is worth remembering that Diana's temple was three and a half times as big. Indeed, it was the largest temple ever constructed in the ancient world.

The original statue of Diana was made of gold, ebony, silver and black stone, but it has long since vanished, along with her great temple. A few slightly later Roman copies in marble do, however, still exist, giving us a fair idea of how she appeared. Diana stood tall and erect, her body festooned with the carved images of animals as though she was in the act of giving birth to the whole of the natural world. She was so demanding that her male priests had to castrate themselves in order to offer her their testicles. As time passed, however, this honour was conveniently transferred to captive bulls. These were brought to a sacrificial altar near her temple where her great effigy, specially decorated for the occasion, was carried to oversee the ceremony in which the huge testicles of the animals were ritually removed, bathed in scented oils and then hung in three rows around her chest. By closely surrounding her with vast quantities of sperm, this procedure was thought to enhance her fertilizing powers; powers that would bring forth not only human offspring, but also animals and crops. It was fervently believed that through her the rich harvests came, bringing affluence to the early agricultural cultures.

The rituals were thought necessary because Diana could not mate in the ordinary way. Since she was seen as the mother of all life, it was felt by her followers that she could not be the mother of specific offspring born to a single father. She was therefore visualized as a virgin goddess, absorbing the male elements she needed through a mystical union with the rows of male organs draped around her towering body. That is why her body is sometimes incorrectly referred to as 'multi-breasted', the rows of castrated bulls' testicles being mistaken for breasts. (It was, incidentally, the legend of the virgin goddess Diana – who saved the world by giving birth to nature – that appears to have inspired the much later legend of the Virgin Mary's immaculate, world-saving delivery.)

Wherever we look in the ancient world we find representations of a Great Mother figure. Her importance was obvious. She commanded great reverence because reproduction was then so revered. But her enormous success was to become the cause of her own downfall. Reproduction of humans, plants and domestic animals was so speeded up that, eventually, the small villages were able to grow into market towns and the towns into great cities. The urban revolution had occurred. There were two unforeseen consequences of this: first, as communities became more and more populous, fecundity became less of a burning need; second, the male role in organizing these new cities became more and more important.

What happened was that the old male hunting groups were converted into new male ruling groups. They focused on a different kind of hunting now; the ritualized hunting we usually refer to as war. Crops still had to be planted, animals bred and babies born, but now there was a new clamour – the din of battle and the clash of metal.

As the males rose to positions of power in the spreading civilizations, something had to give. The deity had to change sex. The Great Mother had to become God the Father, an all-powerful masculine figure more suited to the harsh new world of weapons, dungeons, tortures, battlefields and other manly inventions.

After God 'had the operation', a great deal was lost. Technology advanced, but at a huge price. The new, sterner, belligerent God figures brought with them a new relationship between the sexes. Women lost their high status. For a million years they had been the equal of males – different, but equal – but now they were relegated to a subordinate role. The gender wars had begun.

Women as Possessions

In some cultures, even today, the situation has changed little. Women in certain parts of the world are still treated

One of the surviving statues of Diana of Ephesus (left). The virgin goddess is adorned with several rows of bulls' testicles.

When seen as the possessions of men, women are often required to veil their beauty from the eyes of strangers (below).

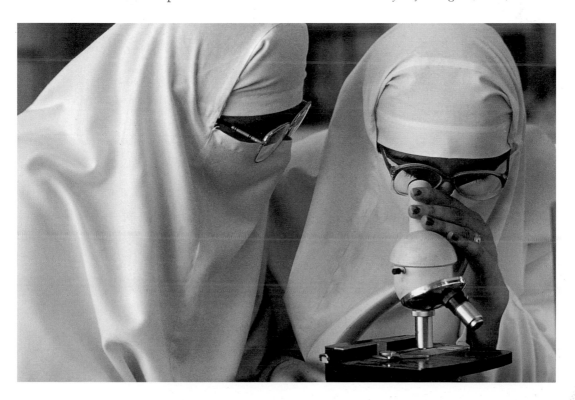

as the possessions of the males and are not allowed to live free lives in the society where they are still expected to give birth and rear the next male-dominated generation. For these women, life holds little in the way of adventure or creativity. Forbidden to show their faces in public, forbidden even in some countries to drive a car, they must live out their existence in a social cocoon, their personal identities publicly erased by their possessive husbands.

These conditions are most commonly encountered in Arab countries, but there is considerable variation in the degree to which the Arab males closet their women and there are many different ways in which the Arab women subordinate themselves to their husbands and to other males.

In the Yemen, for example, women must wait until their men have enjoyed their meals before they themselves can sit down to eat. Even in restaurants they are not allowed to eat with the men and are segregated in a separate room. It may seem odd in such a culture to find that the men do the shopping, but this is simply to ensure that the women remain indoors as much as possible. It is only indoors that the women are allowed to remove their veils and, even there, they must quickly put them on again if male visitors arrive.

For the Yemeni woman who wishes to perform a simple, everyday action like smoking a cigarette, there is a serious problem. She is not allowed to lift her veil to put the cigarette to her lips, nor is she permitted to bore a small hole in the veil through which she could push the tip of the cigarette. Instead she has to smoke *through* the veil, holding the fabric in her mouth and then making a special effort to suck the smoke through it. This is so inconvenient that some females have started to ignore the rule and sneak a puff by surreptitiously lifting their veils, but they risk castigation for such licentious actions.

Special problems arise when women are about to give birth. The hospital staff would like to see them in functional outfits more suited to the occasion, but the most devout among their patients refuse. They insist on continuing to wear the veil, even during the act of delivery itself. This is despite the fact that no male medical official would be allowed to set eyes on the unclad female figure. Even a naked arm is taboo to strange male eyes, so a male gynaecologist has little chance in the Yemen. The mother-to-be may only be attended by female nursing staff.

In Saudi Arabia, wearing the veil is not merely local custom, it is the law, and some women become so conditioned to being covered up that they even sleep in their veils. When they die they are buried wearing their veils.

In public there is a fiercely imposed segregation of the sexes. Since women in Saudi Arabia are not allowed to drive, this creates a problem when females have to be transported. Who can drive the school bus when it is full of little black-veiled girls on their way to their single-sex schools staffed entirely by female teachers and staff? The answer is that the task has to be carried out by an elderly male, who must at all times be accompanied by a female member of his own family.

Recently, in Afghanistan, a regime was imposed that makes even the Saudis look moderate. The fundamentalist Taliban movement, led by a one-eyed peasant mullah – who, it is claimed, will not allow a female voice to reach his ears for fear of pollution – has imposed restrictions on the female population of Kabul that go beyond mere veiling and become near-imprisonment. A young woman is hardly allowed to leave the confines of her house. She is forbidden to undertake any kind of job, forbidden to talk to males, forbidden to listen to any music other than religious songs, forbidden any form of higher education, forbidden any medical examination by a male doctor, forbidden to dance, watch television, visit a cinema or a theatre. If, by accident or design, a woman shows a single hair, or the tiniest patch of bare flesh in public, she is severely punished, usually by receiving a public beating. On a single day in December 1996, no fewer than 225 women were punished in a single day for breaking the Taliban's clothing laws.

A curious feature of the tradition of wearing of the veil is that it has always been assumed to be Muslim in origin, but that is not the case. It was originally introduced by the ancient Assyrians – a singularly cruel and unpleasant culture – as a way of labelling high-status females. Other women, of lower status, were fair game for male advances, but the veiled ones were to be left in peace. Slave girls were specifically forbidden to wear the veil.

The custom was later taken over by male-dominated Muslim countries and adopted as part of their distorted interpretation of the teachings of the Prophet Mohammed. The Prophet himself would certainly not have approved, since he taught that men and women should be treated equally. The Koran states clearly that, 'Women shall with justice have rights similar to those exercised against them'. And he repeatedly stressed that women

For some women the veil becomes a complete covering, a mobile prison that conceals every physical detail from prying eyes (left). Over 100 million women alive today have suffered the mutilation of female circumcision (below). The intention is to eliminate marital infidelity by reducing the potential for sexual pleasure.

should be treated with kindness and fairness. As a result, during the early years of Islam the women went unveiled and often played an active, leading role in society. But such matters are easily forgotten by power-hungry males when they pose as pious religious leaders and seize control of gullibly devout populations. Sadly, there is about as much hope that Mohammed's true teachings regarding women will be reinstated as there is that the Pope will give the treasures of the Vatican away to the poor.

Modern Islamic scholars are themselves quite clear about the role of the veil. They emphasize that, 'There has never been an Islamic obligation for women to cover at any time. In fact, veiling the face is an innovation that has no foundation whatsoever in Islam. Even in Saudi Arabia the covering of women from head to toe is recent; it was not required before the discovery of oil.' This is a much more educated view than the one put forward by early Islamic scholars, who insisted that, 'All of woman is pudendal'. In other words, she is nothing but one huge sexual organ. She is not a women who *has* 'private parts', she *is* a private part, and must, therefore, be completely covered up.

These early teachers of what is right and wrong managed to convince most women that it was honourable and dignified to cover their faces. It prevented unseemly attentions from males – presumably driven mad by the sight of a walking pudendum – and so gave the veiled females the freedom to walk about unaccosted. It never occurred to the early teachers to suggest that males should learn to restrain themselves.

And so it came to be that a form of symbolic slavery for women was sold to society as a form of honourable decorum. Many women bought this explanation and defended their covered condition by saying that, without the veil, they would feel vulgar and shameless. Interestingly, however, for Sir Richard Burton, translator of *The Arabian Nights,* the *presence* of a veil is seen as equally provocative: '…it conceals coarse skin, fleshy noses, wide mouths and vanishing chins, while it sets off to best advantage what is most lustrous and liquid – the eye'. For him, at least, the veil, that 'most coquettish article of women's attire', was a challenge rather than a put-off. If all men were like him, then women would be better protected by *not* wearing a facial covering.

The reality, however, is that for society in general the veil is a clear social message, like a nun's habit, shouting 'keep away', and it labels the wearer as the possession of a male – a possession that must not be touched. It does not seem to occur to the men concerned that their attitude is particularly insulting, implying that, without the veil to make other men shy away, their women would, at the merest male glance, become sexually abandoned. In countries where the veil has been abandoned, this has certainly not been the case. No matter how one tries to argue around it, the fact is that the veil is an advertisement for male domination and always helps to create a one-sided relationship between men and women.

There are worse restrictions than veils, however. In certain regions of the world the subjugation of the human female knows no bounds. As mentioned in Chapter Four, to ensure their passivity many women in the Middle East and parts of Africa have their external genitals removed during childhood, taking from them the pleasures of the bed – pleasures that might give them sufficient courage to rebel against male tyranny.

The anti-sexual nature of the operation was clearly expressed by one of the 'specialists' who carry it out: 'First I examine them intimately. If their clitoris hangs out and arouses them sexually by rubbing against their underwear, then that's the time it should be cut'.

The numbers involved in these sexual mutilations are much higher than most people realize. This is not an exotic oddity of some backwater tribe. This is a major human activity of appalling and needless cruelty, occurring over a wide geographical range. Every year no fewer than two million small girls are held down, screaming, and without receiving any anaesthetic, to have all or part of their external genitals cut away. The cutting instruments are crude, there is little hygiene and there are frequent deaths, but these are always hushed up. Despite the fact that no religion requires this barbarity, it is defended by those who support it with the words, 'Female circumcision is sacred and life without it would be meaningless'.

Because there has been some public questioning of the ritual recently, the mutilators (who make good money out of performing the operation) have banded together and formed a society to protect themselves. They insist that circumcising the young girls is '...an easy way to reduce their sexual promiscuity that would normally lead to friction in the home between husbands and wives'. And they have demanded that their governments impose a fine of half a million dollars on anyone who dares to discuss the matter further in the local media. Medical authorities are, needless to say, fighting this proposal.

In Egypt, where 3000 girls are circumcised every day, the Egyptian Organization of Human Rights has taken the unusual step of suing the leading Muslim theologian there for half a million pounds because of his support for female mutilation. He had issued a *fatwa* against anyone opposing it, saying they deserve to die and referring to the operation as a 'laudable practice that does honour to women'. Since only 15 per cent of the world's population follows Islam, and nobody outside Islam (not to mention many inside Islam) would condone the practice, this means that this amazing man, the Sheikh of Al Azhar, has ordered the death penalty to be carried out on, at the very least, 85 per cent of the entire human race. The mystery is where this holy man gets his authority for his statement, since there is no mention of female circumcision anywhere in the Koran.

The sheikh's supporters reflect his violent posturing. When a female Egyptian reporter asked awkward questions, she was told to shut up or 'I will cut your tongue out and the tongues of those who gave birth to you'. And in a bizarre outburst that is hard to credit, she was also told that if she herself had had her clitoris removed, she might have had a better complexion.

The scale of this outrage against women is vast. It is hard to believe, but it is a fact that there are over a hundred million women alive today who have had all or part of their external genitals cut away when they were young girls. The figures, country by country, are as follows: Nigeria, 33 million; Ethiopia, 24 million; Egypt, 24 million; Sudan, 10 million; Kenya, 7 million; Somalia, 4.5 million.

When faced with this, the male diplomats and politicians of the United Nations and other such impotent organizations take refuge behind convenient phrases like 'showing respect for local traditions and customs'. It is little wonder that they themselves command so little respect.

In rare cases where, despite everything that is done to control her, a circumcised woman from one of these cultures does stray from the marriage bed, her penalty is much more severe than that for the male. The ancient custom of stoning a woman to death for an act of infidelity still survives in certain regions.

It should be stressed that, although the worst examples of the suppression of female freedom tend to occur in Muslim countries, there is nothing in the Muslim religion itself that requires this treatment. As already mentioned, there is no mention of it in the Koran.

Nowhere does it state that women should be veiled, restricted in their movements or circumcised. These are assaults on the liberty of women that have become hallowed by tradition, not by religious doctrine.

Muslim countries are not alone in treating women as second-class citizens. Many Christian countries also restrict them. In Greece, for instance, once women are married they are only permitted to have female friends and they are not allowed in the cafés where men gather.

All over the world, religious practices come to the aid of those who wish to keep male traditions alive. In Thailand, for example, only men can receive enlightenment and women often pray to be reborn as men.

Among strict Jewish sects the subjugation of women entails the complete covering and concealment of a married woman's hair. In preparation for marriage they must have their heads shaved and then, in an amazing example of contradictory thinking, have a special wig of hair made to place over their shaven skulls.

In Japan, age and gender are vitally important in the social order. Expressed simply, older is higher than younger and male is higher than female. Therefore, old males have the highest social standing and young females the lowest. This is reflected in many small details of everyday life.

For example, in Japan a woman cannot pass through a door before a man she considers to be important, even if he politely holds it open for her. An Englishman encountered this when filming in Japan. Nothing he could do would persuade his young female interpreter to pass through the door in front of him, no matter how long he held it open for her. Indeed, she found his misplaced politeness deeply embarrassing. On his way home to England he broke his journey in New York. There, while shopping in Manhattan, he once again held a door open for an approaching female. As he expected, the busy New Yorker did not hesitate and swept past him into the shop. However, as she drew even with him she hissed in his ear, 'Pig!' Once again he had made a mistake, for in New York, battleground of the sexes, his polite gesture had been misinterpreted as an insulting suggestion that women are too weak to open doors for themselves.

This anecdote clearly reveals how the relations between the sexes have reached a confusing stage in social history. Each country has its own rules and it is easy for a traveller to make mistakes. The degree to which the old-style male domination has survived varies enormously.

In the West we congratulate ourselves that we have, at last, removed that tyranny. We even pass laws about sexual equality and equal opportunities. But despite this the shadow of the dominant male still lurks just beneath the surface on social occasions. Sometimes this domination is so familiar that we barely notice it. Take, for example, a formal gathering. As the couples arrive they are announced: Mr and Mrs Smith; Sir John and Lady Jones; Lord and Lady Brown. In each case the woman's own surname is omitted. In its place is her husband's name with a title added. The men may pride themselves on not treating their wives as possessions, but they have nevertheless taken possession of their names.

The genteel atmosphere of the typical Western wedding appears to be balanced enough, with the bride being given just as much importance as the groom. But a closer look at what lies behind the wedding ceremony paints a different picture. Beneath the surface there again lurks the shadow of the dominant male, taking possession of his mate.

For example, the bride is 'given away' by her father. She is passed on, like a piece of property, from the father to the groom, for safekeeping. Nobody gives the groom away. His mother does not lead him into the church and hand him over to the bride for safekeeping. So, from the very beginning, the wedding service is one-sided.

The placing of a wedding ring on the third finger of the bride's left hand is meant to humble her and is a deliberate subordination of her to her husband. The left hand is, by tradition, inferior to the right, and the third finger is used because it has less independence of movement than the other digits. Placing the ring on that particular finger symbolizes the inferiority of the bride and her loss of independent action. In some cultures, despite its early symbolism as a sign of eternity, the wedding ring was seen as a token payment for the bride – 'With this ring I thee purchase'.

It is no accident that the symbolic ring is supplied by the best man, for it was he who was meant to be the strong-arm accomplice who would help the groom in the physical capture of his new wife, if force were needed. Indeed, in early weddings, it was the best man and his male friends who were responsible for bringing not the groom but the bride to the church, to ensure that she did not attempt to escape. Originally it was the task of the bridesmaids to surround the groom and make sure that he arrived safely at the church. Today the roles of the bridesmaids and best man have somehow been switched, which means that their original significance has been lost.

During the wedding service, the bride stands on the left side of the groom. Traditionally, this was so that his strong right arm was ready to attack anyone who interfered with the ceremony. Again, it emphasizes the dominant role of the groom.

The traditional kiss between the bride and groom following the marriage service is a remnant, a modern symbol of sexual consummation. In earlier times, it was required that there should be a display of the blood-stained bridal bedsheets, which were shown to all and sundry as proof of the bride's virginity on her wedding night. In other words, there had to be a public demonstration that the bride was a valuable acquisition – a worthwhile 'property'.

When the couple are about to leave, after the wedding reception, they may find old shoes tied to the back of their getaway car. This harks back to the time when the bride's father would give one of his daughter's old shoes to the groom, who would playfully tap her on the head with it, symbolizing the shift of power over her from her father to her new husband. In other words, the father can now no longer spank his daughter with a slipper when she misbehaves – this is now the duty of the husband. As the couple's car speeds away from the wedding reception with shoes dancing behind it, and tin cans rattling to scare away evil spirits, the parents of the bride finally renounce their control over her and accept that she has now moved on to a new form of ownership.

When the couple finally arrive at their destination, the groom has to carry his bride over the threshold if the marriage is to be a success. Once again, this is a symbol of his power over her and dates back to marriage by capture. It also neatly symbolizes his physical strength and her physical weakness.

So, as they settle down to their wedding night, the Western couple can look back on a series of events during which they have gone to great lengths to emphasize the inequality of the male and female, with the bride is always cast in the subordinate, inferior role. Even the name 'bride' itself is part of this conspiracy, for it is derived from an old word 'brude', from the root 'bru', meaning to brew or to cook. In other words, to be a bride is, by definition, to commit oneself to domestic duties. It is little wonder that today so many couples are ignoring this antiquated pairing display and taking the previously unthinkable step of expressing their love for one another simply by starting to live together. It has to be admitted that, for a culture that pays lip service to sexual equality, the traditional wedding service is hopelessly out of date.

Even after the wedding is over, the ancient practices continue. As the young couple set off on their honeymoon they think of this next phase as a holiday together to relax after the public ordeal they have just gone through; an opportunity to escape from their usual worries and cares and a chance to devote some time to strengthening their love for one another. But again, there is more to it than meets the eye.

Originally, the honeymoon was meant to last for one month or moon, and the couple were expected to drink honey every night, in the form of mead. In times of wife-capture, the idea of the couple being shut away together was to enable the groom to hide his bride from her pursuing family and angry relatives, who were trying to rescue her. This is why, even today, the destination of the honeymooners is meant to be kept secret. If the bride had been forcibly abducted by the groom, his ushers were required to stand guard outside the bridal suite and to repel intruders until her virginity had been taken. At that point she would become worthless to her family, they would depart and the guard could relax.

The length of the honeymoon was intended to enable the groom to make love to his bride throughout a complete menstrual cycle, thus ensuring that he was with her when she ovulated. The honey, traditionally an aphrodisiac, was intended to intensify their sexual activity and in this way to assist in making her pregnant. The continued isolation of the couple, even after the angry relatives had departed, also helped the groom by making certain that it was he and not some other male who fathered their future child. This may sound strange to us today in an era of romantic love-matches where the bride is supposed to have eyes only for her new husband, but in earlier times it was a useful precaution to ensure the desired paternity.

In some countries, there is a less covert, more blatant celebration of the act of obtaining a bride by capture. In Finland there is an annual Wife-Carrying Contest to commemorate a legendary Finnish figure who was notorious for rape, plunder and capture. However, unlike the traditional marriage customs, these proceedings excuse themselves to some extent by being decidedly light-hearted.

The honeymoon (above) is a
'honey-month' during which the
male has sole access to his female
throughout one complete
menstrual cycle and thus ensures
his paternity of any offspring
that may result.
In Finland there is an annual
wife-carrying contest (left)
that re-enacts the wife-capture
of earlier times.

215

The Female Rebellion

In many other aspects of Western life, the female is still treated unfairly when compared with her male counterpart. For example, many legal procedures continue to treat the wife as inferior to the husband. This is one of the reasons why, during the past 40 years, formal marriage has shown such a rapid decline in the West. With the male-dominated State and the male-dominated Church combining forces to keep women in their place (while of course paying lip service to trendy forms of social correctness) it is not surprising that the clear-thinking young have turned their backs on both those hypocritical institutions.

At first the rebellion was not easy. When the movement towards informal pairings first appeared it caused public anger. Children born to couples living 'in sin', as it was quaintly called, were referred to as 'bastards'. But this has now changed and many informal couples exist without any personal qualms or social condemnation. The coy entry on the hotel register reading 'Mr and Mrs Smith' has become increasingly rare. Now a lover is introduced, without embarrassment, simply as 'my partner'.

With some couples, however, there lingers the desire to perform a public display of commitment. They do not wish to go through a traditional church wedding, and have no respect for legal marriage documents, but they do want something to mark their passage into a new social condition. In particular, they want a ceremony that will truly recognize their sexual equality and will not cast the female in a subordinate role. For such couples there are now many different kinds of alternative weddings available.

One example of this genre is the pagan wedding. In California (where else?) it is possible to be married in a pagan ritual by a priestess called Cerridwen Fallingstar, a minister of the Covenant of the Goddess. A shamanic witch, her elaborate ceremonies amalgamate and integrate a whole range of different sacred beliefs including Native American, Afro-Caribbean, New Age, Tantra, Taoist, Reiki and Celtic.

The pagan ceremony begins with the purifying of the guests with burning herbs and the sprinkling of seawater. This is followed by a period of meditation and chanting and the ringing of Tibetan bells. The couple then exchange vows, rings and flowers and share a glass of a sacred drink. Their hands are tied together to symbolize the bond between them and the ceremony ends with the 'jumping of the broom', a phallic interpretation of their passing over the threshold of marriage. After the completion of such a ceremony, the couple feel thoroughly 'paired' but have been able to acquire that condition without submitting to any of the male-dominated rituals of the established Church.

For many modern women, though, the whole concept of marriage, whether formal or informal, has become synonymous with the exploitation of the human female. This poses an interesting question: if women once accepted male 'protection', why have they now started to reject it? How has this new attitude developed? What has given rise to the recent female rebellion against the traditional male domination of society?

There are three reasons. First, the human population levels have risen so high that there is no longer any pressure to produce large families. If this leads to the logical step of reducing family size by sexual abstinence, contraception or abortion, the female is no longer incapacitated by massive maternal demands. Second, advancing technology has robbed the male of his age-old advantage based on superior physical strength – there are few high-status tasks that cannot now be successfully performed by females. Third, there is an increasing surplus of women. It has been estimated that, by the year 2000, there will be a female world surplus of 175 million. Whenever the sex ratio has been tipped in this direction in the past the result has been an upsurge in female activity. (By contrast, whenever men have outnumbered women there has been a tendency for the women to be treated as carefully protected possessions and allowed few if any social freedoms.)

The first wave of rebellion came at the turn of the century with the women's suffrage movement. The second wave appeared in the late 1960s with the feminist movement. In 1966, a group of American activists formed the National Organization for Women, and other groups were quick to follow, both in the United States and in Europe. Some became bogged down in the trivia of social etiquette, but others began to make serious assaults on entrenched attitudes and, little by little, the public stereotypes of women started to change. The main battle was to destroy the concept of the typical adult woman as essentially passive, dependent, and over-emotional. The main aim was to establish the female as an independent figure. In the past, her reliance on the male's pay packet had kept her in a subservient role, and that restriction was soon to come under close scrutiny.

At its most passionate and extreme, the feminist movement became a hymn of hate for all things masculine. This attitude culminated with the formation of SCUM (Society for Cutting Up Men) in New York in 1967. Its manifesto included the following comments:

There have been two main phases of female rebellion: the turn-of-the-century suffrage movement (above), concentrating on political issues; and the 1960s feminist movement (right) focusing more on sexual issues.

[SCUM exists] to overthrow the government, eliminate the money system, institute complete automation and destroy the male sex. It is now technically feasible to reproduce without the aid of males...and to produce females. We must begin immediately to do so...To be male is to be deficient, emotionally limited; maleness is a deficiency disease and males are emotional cripples. The male is completely egocentric, trapped inside himself, incapable of empathizing or identifying with others...He is a half-dead, unresponsive lump, incapable of giving or receiving pleasure or happiness... SCUM will kill all men who are not in the men's auxiliary of SCUM. Men in the men's auxiliary are those men who are working diligently to eliminate themselves...men who kill men...Prior to the institution of automation, to the replacement of men by machines, the male should be of use to the female, wait on her, cater to her slightest whim, obey her every command, be totally subservient to her, exist in perfect obedience to her will...

The tone of this diatribe makes it clear that the human male is a weak enemy on his way to an early extinction. To fully satisfy SCUM it would be necessary to kill every adult male on this planet. In the battlefield of the gender wars, it is impossible to be more extreme than this. Needless to say, with its avowedly criminal platform SCUM did not acquire many recruits. The author of the manifesto, actress Valerie Solanas, did manage to achieve some degree of personal notoriety when, on 3 June 1968, six months after founding SCUM, she shot and seriously wounded the bizarre American artist Andy Warhol. This was a promising start for SCUM but her act of violence did not build the momentum she had hoped for and today the movement is little more than a faint, eccentric memory. Nevertheless, it summed up, in a highly exaggerated form, the general mood of the day, with women in the Western world increasingly reluctant to tolerate the unnatural degree of male dominance in modern society.

The assault on the bastions of masculinity took several routes, some bizarre, some deadly serious and others frankly trivial. The bizarre attacks centred on male sexuality. The more serious campaigns concerned themselves with the unfair treatment of women in the realms of employment, education, economics and legal matters. The trivial onslaughts were directed at minor social customs. I will examine these next.

Female Sexual Freedom

In the realms of sexuality, the female rebellion led to some spectacular excesses, from the Plastercasters of the early 1970s to the Bobbit-mimics of the 1990s. The Plastercasters' objective was to gain access to famous young males, arouse them sexually until they had achieved a full erection and then to encase the erect penis in plaster. Once the plaster (or, to be more precise, the dental cement) had dried, it was removed and used as a mould to create phallic sculptures that could be displayed as trophies. The Plastercasters originally hailed from Chicago, but they travelled all over the United States in their quest for new 'enshrinements', taking their collection of prized casts with them. Among their favourite trophies were the impressive 'effigies' of stars such as Jimi Hendrix, Keith Moon and Jim Morrison.

The young men who were co-opted for this strange project felt strangely flattered by the attention, but overlooked its underlying message, which was that the male phallus was being demystified and 'possessed' by the young women concerned. Gone was the virginal shyness that so arouses male desire. In its place was a blatant sexual boldness, previously the domain of the male stud but now appropriated by the uninhibited females. It was a blow for equality based on the idea that females can be just as sexually rampant as males.

While some males welcomed this concept, others felt threatened by it. The division between them reflected something that had happened to urban sexuality and which was at the root of a great deal of female dissatisfaction. Although they did not display it outwardly, two types of sexual male had arisen in modern urban society. These can be classified, in an over-simplified way, as the *Sexual Giver* and the *Sexual Taker*.

The Givers are those men who have retained the primeval pattern of shared sexual pleasure. During evolution, both the human male and the human female have developed a powerfully erotic response to sexual stimulation that has gone far beyond mere procreation. It has become one of the main binding devices that cements the relationship between human couples, helping to keep them together as a breeding, double-parental unit. It operates on the basis of each partner giving maximum sexual pleasure to the companion, leading in ideal circumstances to that most intense form of 'emotional bonder', the simultaneous orgasm.

The essence of human eroticism of this kind is that it is based on a perfectly balanced sexual equality, in which each partner's primary concern is giving pleasure, rather than taking it. It is the evolutionary solution to keeping the human family together as a long-term breeding unit. It employs physical lust as the primary mechanism of emotional love.

The most significant feature of this reciprocal giving is that it sees women in a role that is just as sexually active as men, so the arrival of the liberated female did not make the male Giver feel threatened by the demand for sexual equality. He already accepted it in private and welcomed it when it was made public.

The position was very different for the male Taker. He had become an increasingly common phenomenon in modern society – the male who 'scored', who took his pleasure when he felt like it and treated his women as little more than elaborate masturbation devices. A proponent of the 'wham-bang-roll-over' school of sexual finesse, he had abandoned the ancient eroticism of his species and replaced it with a monkey-like insertion-and-climax. His sole aim was to find a female passive enough to accept his phallus

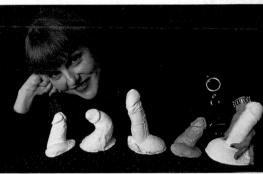

The female rebellion has brought much greater sexual freedom for modern women. This is symbolized by the outrageous activities of the Plastercasters from Chicago, who made a collection of celebrity phalluses (above) and by the increasing popularity of male striptease (left).

and to lie still long enough for him to obtain a quick ejaculation. No thought of sexual pleasure or active involvement for the female even entered his head. Women were simply there to be taken, so he took them, and later wondered why he found something missing from his emotional life.

To be fair to the Taker, he was encouraged to some extent by an insidious propaganda that had been spread by prudish moralizers, which suggested that it was 'unladylike' for women to enjoy sex. The girl who was told to 'lie still and think of England' was no fiction. She was all too real. Indoctrinated with the idea that sex was a nasty duty, she drove men to be both Takers and, ultimately, adulterers. Her prediction that 'all men are selfish brutes' became a self-fulfilling prophecy. In the end, the female rebellion was as much against her as against the brutish male.

The new, liberated attitude towards female sexual behaviour met resistance from both the callous male Taker and the frigid female prude. The idea of active female lust was hard for either of them to accept. And the idea that this might represent the true biological inheritance of the human female had never occurred to them. They saw the openly erotic females as an outrageous modern decadence and a danger to the established pattern of family life. In reality, of course, it was the prim, passive females who were the real danger, driving their men to seek fulfilment elsewhere.

Clawing back their active sexuality was a difficult task for the liberated females, and they were not helped by a division within their own ranks. There were those who genuinely wanted a return to the natural balance of the sexes, with joyously, equally shared male and female sexuality, and there were those who simply wanted to crush and humiliate men and all they stood for. Unfortunately for the female liberation movement, it was women who had been badly hurt by men, and who were therefore driven to seek some kind of revenge, that were attracted in numbers to the new feminist cause. They were at war and men were the enemy that had to be destroyed.

In their anger with all that was male, these women turned to sexual alternatives – to celibacy, to lesbian love, or to masturbation. They abandoned all forms of feminine display, adopting a drab appearance almost as sexless as that of nuns. They opposed anything to do with female 'allure' or beauty, claiming that it was pandering to male domination and overlooking the fact that it also had something to do with female sexuality.

While these extremists were able, through tireless dedication to their cause, to reduce some of the worst male excesses, they did little to regain the active, primeval sexuality of the human female. As a result, their campaign was strangely one-sided. As time passed, however, the serious gains they had made on behalf of their gender became beneficially absorbed into the culture and managed to survive long after the damage caused by their initial vitriol had faded. Sexual display returned to the female form and sexual joy to the female partner, but now on an equal footing with the primeval balance between the sexes restored.

Although this was true for many couples in the West, there were major exceptions to the rule. The powerful wave of change lost its momentum as it spread out from the great cities into the small towns and villages of the countryside. And it petered out altogether before it reached the shores of the (ironically misnamed) 'developing world', where male-dominated traditions survived virtually untouched. The result today is a world where every conceivable variation of gender balance is in operation, from liberated female equality to what can only be described as female near-enslavement.

Another side issue has recently emerged. With female liberation has come a new response to female abuse. Female retaliatory violence has shown a marked increase. The battered wife has been joined in the gallery of social types by the battered husband. Hostile, cruel or callous males are no longer able to humiliate their female partners without fear of reprisal. The watershed case was the attack on an American husband called Wayne Bobbit in 1993. His wife, Lorena, pushed to the limit by his churlish behaviour, finally responded by picking up a knife and cutting off his penis as he lay sleeping. Driving away from the scene afterwards, she threw the severed organ from her car window. It was later found and successfully stitched back in place. Photographs of its successful reinstatement were later shown on television and its owner became, if only briefly, a celebrity.

The Bobbit case opened up a new channel for female self-expression. The assault on that symbol of male domination, the phallus, escalated from the benignly amusing world of the 1970s plastercasters to the savage butchery of the 1990s Bobbit-mimics. For Lorena Bobbit has unintentionally created a new fashion in female revenge. Men who fail to respond to the new climate of gender relations are now liable to be treated to a short, sharp shock by their sexual partners.

Bobbit-mimic cases are rare, but they are increasing, especially in countries where male chauvinism remains rampant. One such country is Brazil, where a man can still escape punishment for killing a woman if he can prove that she has in some way 'damaged his honour'. There has recently been a wave of attacks by Brazilian women on the genitals of their male partners. The most famous is the Mattos case, in which a young grocer was attacked by his schoolgirl lover. Following a night of love in a hotel room, he announced that he was leaving her. She responded by pulling him into a close embrace, picking up a sharp knife and hacking off his penis. With great presence of mind he plunged the severed organ into an ice bucket and phoned the police. After a four-hour operation, he and his favourite extremity were successfully reunited. It was later announced by the Macho Society of Brazil that Mattos would receive the organization's annual award for 'the most macho man in the country'. The very fact that such an organization exists and that Brazilian feminists have now set up a Guillotine Movement to support female castrators, gives some idea of the giant problems ahead for amicable gender relations in that country.

Mattos was not the only victim. When a drunken farm labourer called Geraldo Fagundes tried to rape his wife, she sliced off his left testicle and, for good measure, flushed it down the toilet. Another man, whose adultery had just been discovered by his partner, suffered a partially severed penis. And another, who came home with telltale lipstick marks on his clothing, suffered severe burns when his partner threw boiling water over his genitals. Most savage of all was the case of the outraged woman who tore off her partner's penis with her bare hands. It is reported that Brazilian males have recently developed the habit of sleeping on their stomachs.

Brazil is not alone in this. In Britain recently there was a case of a betrayed woman who melted down all the candles she could find in the house and then threw the pan of boiling wax over her sleeping husband's crotch. The skin surface of the entire middle section of his body was destroyed. The sexual wrath of the disaffected female is clearly not on the wane.

Female Social Equality

In the 1950s the American physiologist Gregory Pincus developed an oral contraceptive for women that successfully suppressed ovulation. This revolutionary birth-control pill became publicly available in 1960. At a modest cost of no more than $11 a month it enabled women, for the first time in history, to govern their own breeding rate. Then, in 1973, the Supreme Court in the United States legalized abortion. Now women, like men, could enjoy sexual liaisons without having to face the risk of long-term biological consequences.

During the years that followed, women continued to make wide use of the birth-control pill but then, in 1996, a new threshold was passed. For years Catholics had been told that the only acceptable form of contraception was the 'natural rhythm method', in which couples kept a note of the dates of the woman's cycle and avoided the days in and around the time of ovulation. By making love only in the safe periods, just before and just after menstruation, it was possible for a couple to avoid pregnancy without any 'artificial' aid, that is to say, any chemical or mechanical forms of contraception.

The problem with the rhythm method is that it is prone to inaccuracy, especially if a woman's cycle is irregular. But in October 1996 a new system of checking 'safe days' was made available to the public for the first time, an ingenious device that adds the refinements of modern technology to this traditional method.

A small, hand-held monitor is activated simply by pressing a button on the day that the menstrual flow starts. Then, each morning, the woman checks the colour of a small light on the monitor box. If it is green, she is safe; if it is yellow, she carries out a simple urine test. A stick supplied with the monitor is moistened with her urine and inserted into the monitor, causing either a red or a green light to show. On six to 10 days out of the whole monthly cycle, the red one will glow, indicating that it is unsafe to make love. On all other days it is perfectly safe to do so.

This improved, technical version of the old 'rhythm method' means that women now have an added advantage. If they prefer not to take chemical control pills, or any other form of contraception, they can go through a normal cycle, ovulate in the usual way, and still enjoy unfettered sexual activity for at least two-thirds of the month. With this and an improved 'morning after' pill on the horizon, the scene is now set for complete sexual equality with regards to the biological consequences of sexual encounters.

In response to Professor Higgins' famous question in *My Fair Lady*, 'Why can't a woman be more like a man?', now, at last, they can. Deciding when and when not to breed is in their hands. They are free to pursue any career they want, regardless of their religious affiliation. They can avoid motherhood without giving up sex. They can play men at their own game.

This trend has in fact been gaining momentum for several decades, ever since the first introduction of the birth-control pill. And in the West, at least, it shows no sign of abating. Before long, the problem arose as to how to make good use of this new status. One answer was to change the whole structure of society, to make it more female-friendly. Inevitably, this would prove to be a very long-term project. Like Rome, complicated social structures are not built in a day. In the meantime, since men have been running society, women would have to behave like men. It might not suit them in every way, but it was the only route open to them in the short term if they were to obtain the social equality that their new sexual equality permitted.

A great deal of serious work has been done in the fields of law and economics which reveals that, although the female workforce, viewed globally, is responsible for two-thirds of the total number of hours worked, it only receives 10 per cent of the world's total income and owns only one per cent of the world's property. Unfair discrimination against women on the basis of their gender has been attacked in areas such as property rights, employment and salary levels and many advances have been made in the second half of the twentieth century, at least in Western society. Menstruating women may still not be allowed to enter Balinese temples, but in the West women have been able to invade almost all the old bastions of male supremacy. Apart from men's public toilets and a few exclusive clubs for senile gentlemen there is little left for them to conquer outside the realm of physical sports.

Even with sports they are beginning to make inroads, although not usually in direct competition with the inevitably more muscular males. Women's wrestling and even women's boxing are fast-growing trends, especially in Japan and the United States.

Japanese women's pro-wrestling is experiencing a boom in popularity, reflecting the new image of 'attractive but tough' that is typical of the increasingly liberated young woman of Japan. The names of the wrestlers give a hint of the mood of the events: top favourites include such daunting figures as 'Sweet Killer', 'Shout the Guts', 'Mighty Transistor' and 'Rush and Beat'. The audience is no longer made up exclusively of men vicariously enjoying the beating up of the loser in a bout, but also of women cheering on their heroine who is triumphantly winning the bout.

In the United States the unthinkable has happened (unthinkable, that is, to the male-dominated sporting world). Mixed wrestling has surfaced. In 24 of the 50 states this is now officially permitted. In the others it is still forbidden. Texas is one of the states that forbids it and it is there that two teenage female wrestlers recently sued their school authorities for $10,000 for preventing them from taking part in the State Finals. The two girls had shown themselves to be worthy opponents and, when wrestling in states where mixed wrestling is permitted, had proved that they could beat boys.

In the great American tradition, the authorities are, at the time of writing, countersuing the girls, claiming that mixed matches could lead to the schools being accused of promoting sexual harassment. Even in the notoriously over-imaginative world of American litigation, it is hard to keep a straight face when confronted with such a desperate defence. And their second argument, that the safety of the girls is at risk because the boys are physically stronger, is equally ludicrous. It overlooks the fact that these school wrestling matches are age-restricted and that teenage girls are at a more advanced growth stage than boys of the same age. It also overlooks the fact that amateur wrestling, unlike professional 'theatrical' wrestling, relies as much upon agility and quick thinking as it does on muscle power.

If anyone is at risk in these mixed sex encounters it is the boys. To be beaten by a girl could seriously damage their male egos, and, if they found the groping and grappling sexually arousing they could also be damaged elsewhere if suddenly thrown to the ground with a full erection.

Women's boxing has also met with great resistance from the male sporting authorities. Four arguments have been levelled against it: (1) women have a lighter bone structure; (2) women have more delicate skin; (3) women have breasts that can be damaged by direct punching; and (4) it is unfeminine to box.

Despite these objections, it is slowly gaining acceptance. In 1993 the Women's International Boxing Federation was formed and a year later staged the first ever women's professional boxing event in Europe at London's York Hall in Bethnal Green. This was an all-female event but, as yet, male boxing authorities in Europe have not permitted female bouts to be included on the bill at male events. That stage will undoubtedly come, and

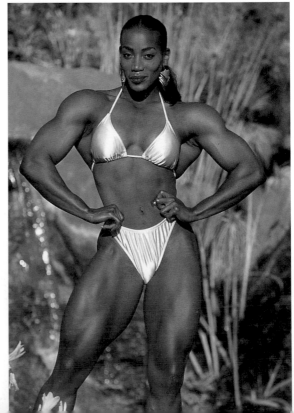

The female rebellion has enabled modern women to engage in a much wider range of activities, including boxing (above), body-building (right) and wing-walking (far right). High-risk activities, previously thought to be the preserve of the male, are now open to both sexes.

indeed has already arrived in the United States where female boxing has recently become commonplace.

How does female boxing defend itself against its critics? The counter-argument to the claim about delicate bone and skin is that women do not punch as hard as men, so the equation balances out. The damage to breasts is sometimes prevented by the wearing of breast protectors and, even when these are not worn, as one female boxer commented, 'You are not going to knock someone out by hitting their breasts, are you? You just really don't hit there.' This only leaves the argument about femininity, which is purely a matter of opinion. It is undeniably unfeminine to use a urinal or shave your chin, but how can it be said that one person hitting another has any intrinsic gender bias? The bias is entirely a matter of social convention and that is precisely what the female rebellion is setting out to change.

It has been suggested that a better way of achieving sexual equality in the noble art of boxing would be for both sexes to stop doing it. However, as there is no sign of the male sport declining in favour, despite repeated criticism from the medical profession, the only solution for women demanding sexual equality in all walks of life is to 'join the boys'. One commentator pointed out that it is rather sad that, just because men are foolish enough to want to be boxers, bullfighters or priests, women feel that they too must punch one another in the face, torture large animals or perpetuate ancient superstitions. Simply because a role has been exclusively male does not mean that there is any great advance for women in mimicking it.

Perhaps the most extraordinary example of women joining the female rebellion by adopting male fighting techniques concerns a group of nuns in Asia. In recent years Catholic sisters following their calling in India have made themselves extremely unpopular locally by trying to persuade low-caste Hindus to convert to Christianity. This has annoyed middle-caste Hindus and there have been savage attacks on nuns by Hindu fanatics throughout the country. Among the outrages one nun was stabbed to death by a gang in Central India, five more were battered with iron bars by masked intruders who broke into a convent near New Delhi and another was raped at knifepoint in Rajasthan. The obvious solution was to turn to the police but, as one nun pointed out, 'When a sister is gang-raped by officers in a police station where can she turn?'

The sisters of St Anne's Convent in Madras decided enough was enough. Without giving up their vows or their austere and pious lifestyle, they set out to become proficient in the art of self-defence. If the law would not help them, they would help themselves. The Mother Superior of St Anne's approached a Muslim karate master by the name of Shihan Hussaini and he agreed to assist them. Forty-five of the sisters enrolled and began an intensive course of instruction. One of his first lessons was to teach them that pain was their friend. He did this by making them lie down in a row and then riding a motorcycle over their hands. Every morning after prayers they were given a 20-minute session during which they became proficient at breaking tiles with hand-chops and head-butts. Many of the sisters can now smash a stack of as many as five tiles with their bare hands. They were also trained in the fine art of attacking the weak points of their assailants' bodies, including the thrusting of a knee into an attacker's groin. This assault on male genitals seems somewhat out of keeping with the image of a devout nun, but one sister explained reassuringly that, 'All the movements can be done with modesty', although she did not explain how.

The most bizarre example of sisterly aggression concerns the way they were taught to hold a metal crucifix in the palm of one hand, with the sharp upper point protruding through their clenched fingers. Using the crucifix as a knuckle-duster in this way provided them with a holy weapon of startling efficiency. This may not have been orthodox Christian practice, and it is hard to reconcile it with Christ's teaching about turning the other cheek, but it did at least enable these remarkable women to carry out their sacred duties of caring for the most wretched members of the local community. They now wear red karate badges pinned to their habits as a warning to would-be thugs. As one sister put it, 'Forgiveness…is still there, but these are changing times. I can turn one cheek, a second cheek, but where is my third cheek?' In the past her rapist attackers could probably have answered that anatomical question all too well, but it is doubtful whether, in the future, they will be in any condition to do so.

All over the world, the newly liberated female is challenging her male counterparts. Men, as part of their adaptation to a primeval hunting life, evolved a stronger inclination for risk-taking, so women now do likewise. The daredevil female has been born.

Nothing is too dangerous. One of the most spectacular female pursuits today is wing-walking. In this, a young woman climbs on top of the upper wing of a biplane and connects herself to a vertical metal post. Attached in this way, she is free to rotate her body and can completely invert it while her pilot loops the loop and performs other aerobatics. In the west of England, wing-walker Helen Tempest has been giving displays in this way for several years, taking to the skies almost every day for a joyously symbolic expression of twentieth-century female freedom. In her most daring exploit she shook hands with a fellow wing-walker who was standing on another aeroplane. To achieve this, one bi-plane had to fly along upside-down, a few feet above the other, with the risk that any sudden gust of wind could have instantly created a crushed wing-walker sandwich.

Six thousand miles away, in California, other macho females are also airborne, this time in a more serious role against a more sombre backdrop. As official fire-fighters they are dropped by parachute into the centre of the state's notorious and all-too-frequent bush fires, where they take equal risks alongside the men.

The Return of the Mother Goddess

Instead of indulging in pseudo-masculine physical activities, some females have fostered a return to the spiritual past when the Great Mother ruled the planet. In some parts of the world, this tradition has never really died out. In Colombia, for example, there still exist the all-powerful shamans called the *cantalores*, who act as spiritual advisers. And in Singapore there is Kuan Ying, the Goddess of Mercy, who continues to wield a strong influence over the local people.

Even in the male-dominated Catholic countries there is a subtle form of rebellion that the male priests find hard to oppose. In many towns and cities it is not Jesus Christ who is the centre of local worship, but his mother, the Holy Virgin. This is allowed because of her close relationship with the official Son of God, but in reality, perhaps unconsciously, the faithful who laboriously and painfully walk to their local church on their knees to pay homage to the Virgin Mary have returned, if only slightly, to the age-old Mother Goddess religion. The Christian Virgin has once again taken on the mantle of the Holy Mother.

In a less serious, but none the less symbolic context, there was strong objection to the casting of a woman to play the role of God in the 1996 York Mystery Plays, the

The 'mother goddess' is still with us in one form or another. In some countries the Virgin Mary (above) is treated almost as a female deity. In others, the Voodoo priestess holds sway. (below).

234

medieval play cycle that is still performed (in a stage version) every four years. A local archdeacon, clearly ignorant of the early Mother Goddess phase of religious beliefs, described this decision by the play's producer as 'political correctness gone mad'. The producer, perhaps in placatory mood, then proceeded to cast a woman (alongside a man) in the counter-balancing role of the Devil. If he felt this would calm the angry clergy, he was probably being optimistic. And, as it happens, he was as mistaken as the archdeacon because, although God was once a woman – and for a much longer period than She has been a He – the Devil has always been male. This is because, in origin, the Devil is the demonized Christian version of the very masculine, protective Horned God of earlier epochs.

In some circles there has been a widespread return to active witchcraft: it has been estimated that in the San Francisco area alone there are at present no fewer than 5000 practising witches. These are not the *Macbeth* variety, however, and they stress that they have no link whatever with evil, the Devil, or the powers of darkness. They are more concerned with healing than with casting spells that cause harm. They see themselves as heralding a return to the Old Religion, which some of them call by the Old English name of Wicca, in which nature is revered, the Earth is considered sacred and the female deity is accepted as the dominant force. This return to the Mother Goddess phase of religion has inevitably found fertile ground among environmentalists and feminists and is now gaining in momentum.

The modern witches are at pains to point out that their 'bad press' was the result of grotesquely unfair and cruel persecution by the early Christian Church. In order to suppress the popular Old Religion, which saw sex as pleasurable and women as worthy of positions of power and prominence, the male authorities of the Christian Church sought to denigrate it. They did this by suggesting that witches were in league with evil spirits, at a time when people were intensely superstitious and went in mortal fear of such forces.

In the fifteenth century the Pope issued an edict that started three centuries of persecution, during which nine million people were sent to painful deaths, either in the flames, at the end of a rope, or after prolonged and hideous torture. All this was done in the name of a loving, forgiving Christ by holy men whose actions were a disgrace to their creed. In order to obliterate the competition from the Old Religion of Europe, they not only set out to persecute and destroy all its practitioners, but also attacked its beliefs. This meant that they were forced to denigrate women and sexual pleasure. Their position became one of virginal purity. The only men and women worthy of a true spiritual existence were those who, like monks and nuns, rejected all sexual pleasures. All other humans, by virtue of their inability to take this holy vow of abstinence, were inferior beings to be pitied and treated like naughty children.

The big problem for this approach to life, which would have come as a shock to Christ had he lived to see it, was that, along with wicked sexual pleasure, it also removed the ability of the human species to reproduce itself. This little difficulty was solved by allowing that the absolute minimum of sexual activity – just enough to procreate more little Christians – was permissible, if regrettable. Since it was women who were concerned with the messily animalistic business of menstruation, pregnancy, birth and breast-feeding, it was they who were seen as further from the sacred condition than men. So they had to become second-class citizens in the eyes of the Church. Their attraction for men was summed up in the saying, 'Women are demons that make us enter Hell through the doors of Paradise'. In other words, their appeal could not be denied but, by giving in to it, men were forced to lower themselves to the bestial level of their carnal partners.

The beleaguered women, who had already lost out badly in the social changes accompanying the urban revolution, now had this added cross to bear. Although witch-burning came to an end in the seventeenth century, the echoes and remnants of their de-valuing were everywhere. They were still required to be sexually modest, as though copulation was something they really disliked and suffered only as a marital duty. And they were widely referred to as 'the weaker sex', 'the softer sex', 'the inferior sex', 'a necessary evil' and even, by Tennyson, as 'the lesser man'. In the eighteenth century, in one of his letters to his son, Lord Chesterfield commented, 'Women are to be talked to as below men, but above children'. Even more extreme, in the seventeenth century, was Thomas Dekker: 'Women, at best, are bad…Were there no women, man might live like gods'.

This was the hidden agenda that the feminists had to combat. Superficially, they were fighting practical matters of men being legally and socially favoured over women. But beneath the surface, the anti-spiritual, animal-natured Great Mother was lurking as the ultimate enemy of the lofty male. So the return of the witch in her original, non-fiendish

For many modern women, the ultimate goal
is to achieve the social equality that sees
them fairly treated in employment, with
a dominant role in business (above)
determined on merit rather than gender.
For others it is important to see a return to
a religious equality such as the ordaining
of women priests (right).

role is less of an eccentric oddity than it might seem. Unfortunately, it has not been handled too well. The very use of the word 'witch' is a poor judgement, since that was the word most strongly associated with the suppression of spiritual females. It is almost as if the new witches *want* to be persecuted all over again. If they hope to make any serious headway as a movement they will have to look back at the Old Religion and find in it those elements that were not too badly demonized by centuries of cruel persecution.

One group, related to the new witches, is the Dianic Cult in California. Their movement appears to be thriving, with high priestesses and an enthusiastic all-female following. They focus exclusively on goddess worship and they stage special ceremonies at which they perform the 'Spiral Dance of the Earth Spirit', complete with magic rituals. Although most of their actions are positive, they do also employ negative elements, unlike some of the other 'new witch' groups. For example, they will put a public curse on rapists or serial killers of women. Victims of male crime are encouraged to do likewise. Dianic Cult members claim they have been able to cause rapists to have car accidents or to be caught the next time they try to commit an offence.

A few centuries ago all the members of these 'alternative cults' would have been burned as witches by the Christian Church, but today they have gained the freedom to express themselves without any hint of persecution. However, they remain very much outside the mainstream of organized religion.

A different approach has been adopted by certain other women, who recently took the step of joining the men in their own camp. They have managed to persuade the Christian Church to abandon its centuries-old male tradition and start to ordain female priests. Perhaps this is not sufficiently confrontational for the followers of Wicca. But whichever way the battle flows, whether by take-over or by open rebellion, in the end the result may well be that spiritual women once again become a major force within the sphere of world religion. Helping this process along is the fact that an increasingly environmentally conscious public is beginning to appreciate once more the nurturing power of Mother Earth. Who knows, perhaps one day the Holy Father in Rome will be replaced by a Holy Mother, and the cycle will be complete…

The Equality of the Sexes

The changes we observe today in the role of women in society have been attributed to the pressures exerted by the women's movements. The members of these movements feel that what they are seeing is a fulfilment of a new philosophy that gives the female, for the first time, a true equality with the male. The truth, however, is rather different. Throughout the million years of our evolutionary past, right up to the point where ancient civilizations arose, tribal males and females must have been of equal social importance. They depended upon one another in a social partnership that demanded equality. Then, as the great urban story began to unfold, females were relegated to a secondary role. Women could not join men in the new workplace. The men took the centre of society away from the tribal home and made it their own. The women were left stranded inside their breeding nests.

Now the need to breed has been lessened and there are techniques readily available to avoid pregnancy. The females can once again enjoy full equality with the males. But it is a new kind of equality. The old equality was based on the fact that heavy maternal duties did not marginalize the females and cast them out to the fringes of society. Indeed, it was the males' hunting lives that marginalized *them*. The females, despite their maternal duties, remained at the very centre of society.

Today, the females have regained their central role, not by restructuring society but simply by leaving the home and joining the males in the new workplace. This allows them to demonstrate their equality in intelligence, ambition and energy, but it leaves them with one major disadvantage. Despite the overcrowding of modern life, and the nightmare statistics of human overpopulation, the maternal urges deep inside many modern females are still strong. The nature of many work-patterns clash with the need to produce even a single child, and for the women of the future this is the principal problem that remains to be solved.

In the meantime, males and females can, in theory, work alongside one another in a balanced relationship based on talent rather than gender, with the battle of the sexes finally relegated to history. In practice, this may take a little while, because old entrenched positions are hard to shift. But the conditions are right for a new era of male and female relationships, with the strength of the male and the stamina of the female combining to create perhaps the most exciting chapter yet in the history of our remarkable species.

Afterword

This book has been written to accompany a documentary television series. If the choice of imagery has sometimes seemed idiosyncratic, this is because the written text has to a large degree followed the visual examples of that series.

The final image of the series was presented as a metaphor for male and female co-operation. It shows a man and a woman helping one another to scale the heights of a vertical rock face in the Yosemite National Park in the United States. Each climber has a special advantage over the other – the male has greater physical strength and the woman has greater physical flexibility and a lighter body. These differences equip them with a genuine equality in their long haul to the top, so that their mutual aid is perfectly balanced. By helping one another as much as they can, they considerably reduce the difficulties they face in their hazardous ascent.

In the best of times, the everyday relationship between a man and a woman is like this. This is how we evolved and it explains our amazing success story as a species.

Today, however, we have no guarantees. If the structure of society permits it, this is how it will be. But if the structure of society becomes warped by our own success, then the relationship between the human couple will suffer. We are so far from our simple tribal beginnings now that our primeval genetic programming may not be able to come to our assistance. Our high intelligence has built us our complex civilizations and it is our high intelligence that must now solve the problems that beset our primal couple.

The pessimist will say that it is too late, that we have broken too many natural rules. The optimist will counter that. if our intelligence created our problems, it will certainly be able to solve them. The realist will say: maybe.

Climbers in Yosemite National Park in the United States. The strength of the male body and the flexibility of the female body makes the mixed couple the perfect combination for a joint ascent to the summit of the great rock-face.

Bibliography

ADAMS, A.L., *Notes of a Naturalist in the Nile Valley and Malta.* Edmonston & Douglas, Edinburgh, 1870. (For the origin of the Maltese Cross)

ANGELOGLOU, M., *A History of Make-up.* Macmillan, London, 1965.

ARCHER, J. & LLOYD, B., *Sex and Gender.* Penguin, Harmondsworth, 1982.

BADCOCK, C., *Oedipus in Evolution.* Blackwell, Oxford, 1990.

BAKER, R., *Sperm Wars.* Fourth Estate, London, 1996.

BAKER, R.R. & BELLIS, M.A., *Human Sperm Competition.* Chapman & Hall, London, 1995.

BARDWICK, J.M., *Psychology of Women; a Study of Bio-cultural Conflicts.* Harper & Row, New York, 1971.

BARING, A. & CASHFORD, J., *The Myth of the Goddess.* Penguin, Harmondsworth, 1991.

BASSERMANN, L., *The Oldest Profession: a History of Prostitution.* Arthur Barker, London, 1965.

BATTEN, M., *Sexual Strategies: How Females Choose Their Mates.* Putnam's, New York, 1992.

BETTELHEIM, B., *Symbolic Wounds: Puberty Rites and the Envious Male.* Thames & Hudson, London, 1955.

BIGELOW, J., *The Joy of Uncircumcising.* Hourglass Book Publishing, California, 1992.

BILLINGTON, S. & GREEN, M., *The Concept of the Goddess.* Routledge, London, 1996.

BRADDOCK, J., *The Bridal Bed.* Robert Hale, London, 1960.

BRAIN, R., *Friends and Lovers.* Hart-Davis, MacGibbon, London, 1976.

BROBY-JOHANSEN, R., *Body and Clothes.* Faber & Faber, London, 1966.

BROCKETT, L.P., *Woman: Her Rights, Wrongs, Privileges and Responsibilities.* Books for Libraries Press, New York, 1869.

CARR, D., *The Sexes.* Doubleday, New York, 1970.

CHANCE, M.R.A., 'Reason for Externalization of the Testis of Mammals' in *Journal of Zoology*, Vol. 239, pp. 691–695. Zoological Society, London, 1996.

CHAPMAN, J.D., *The Feminine Mind and Body.* Vision Press, London, 1967.

CHERFAS, J. & GRIBBIN, J., *The Redundant*

Male. Pantheon Books, New York, 1985.

COOK, M. & WILSON, G., *Love and Attraction*. Pergamon Press, Oxford, 1979.

CORBALLIS, M.C., *The Lopsided Ape*. Oxford University Press, Oxford, 1991.

DANIÉLOU, A., *The Phallus: Sacred Symbol of Male Creative Power*. Inner Traditions, Vermont, 1995.

DAVIES, M. et al., *Humankind the Gatherer-Hunter*. Myddle-Brockton, Swanley, Kent, 1992.

DE BEAUVOIR, S., *The Second Sex*. Jonathan Cape, London, 1953.

DEVINE, E., *Appearances: A Complete Guide to Cosmetic Surgery*. Piatkus, Loughton, Essex, 1982.

DINGWALL, E.J., *The Girdle of Chastity*. Routledge, London, 1931.

EBENSTEN, H., *Pierced Hearts and True Love; the History of Tattooing*. Verschoyle, London, 1953.

EBIN, V., *The Body Decorated*. Thames & Hudson, London, 1979.

FIELDING, W.J., *Strange Customs of Courtship and Marriage*. Souvenir Press, London, 1961.

FISHER, H., *The Sex Contract*. Morrow, New York, 1982.

FISHER, H., *Anatomy of Love*. Norton, New York, 1992.

FORD, C.S. & BEACH, F.A., *Patterns of Sexual Behaviour*. Eyre & Spottiswoode, London, 1952.

FRIDAY, N., *The Power of Beauty*. Hutchinson, London, 1996.

FRIEDAN, B., *The Feminine Mystique*. Norton, New York, 1963.

FRIEZE, I.H. et al., *Women and Sex Roles*. Norton, New York, 1978.

FRYER, P., *Mrs Grundy: Studies in English Prudery*. Dobson, London, 1963.

GHESQUIERE, J. et al., *Human Sexual Dimorphism*. Taylor & Francis, London, 1985.

GLASS, L., *He Says, She Says*. Piatkus, London, 1992.

GLYNN, P., *Skin to Skin: Eroticism in Dress*. Allen & Unwin, London, 1982.

GOFFMAN, E., *Gender Advertisements*. Macmillan, London, 1976.

GRANT, L., *Sexing the Millennium*. Harper Collins, London, 1993.

GREENSTEIN, B., *The Fragile Male*. Boxtree, London, 1993.

GREER, G., *The Female Eunuch*. MacGibbon & Kee, London, 1970.

GUTTENTAG, M. & SECORD, P.F., *Too Many Women?* Sage Publications, Beverly Hills, California, 1983.

HALLET, J P., *Pygmy Kitabu*. Souvenir Press, London, 1973.

HARDIMENT, C., *Perfect Parents*. Oxford University Press, Oxford, 1995.

Bibliography

HASTE, H., *The Sexual Metaphor*. Harvester Wheatsheaf, New York, 1993.

HENNIG, J-L., *The Rear View*. Souvenir Press, London, 1995.

HOWELLS, K., *The Psychology of Sexual Diversity*. Blackwells, Oxford, 1984.

HUTT, C., *Males and Females*. Penguin Books, Middlesex, 1972.

KAMPEN, N.B., *Sexuality in Ancient Art*. Cambridge University Press, Cambridge, 1996.

KEY, M. R., *Male/Female Language*. Scarecrow Press, New Jersey, 1975.

KNIGHT, R.P. & WRIGHT, T., *Sexual Symbolism: A History of Phallic Worship*. Julian Press, New York, 1962.

KUPFERMANN, J., *The MsTaken Body*. Robson Books, London, 1979.

LANG, T., *The Difference Between a Man and a Woman*. Michael Joseph, London, 1971.

LEVY, H.S., *Chinese Footbinding*. Neville Spearman, London, 1963.

LEWINSOHN, R., *A History of Sexual Customs*. Longmans, Green, London, 1958.

LLOYD, B. & ARCHER, J., *Exploring Sex Differences*. Academic Press, London, 1976.

LYNDON, N., *No More Sex War*. Mandarin, London, 1992.

MACCOBY, E.E., *The Development of Sex Differences*. Tavistock, London, 1967.

MANTEGAZZA, P., *The Sexual Relations of Mankind*. Eugenics Publishing, New York, 1935.

MEAD, M., *Male and Female*. Penguin, Harmondsworth, 1962.

MILLER, J.B., *Toward a New Psychology of Women*. Penguin Books, Middlesex, 1976.

MOIR, A. & JESSEL, D., *Brainsex: The Real Difference Between Men and Women*. Mandarin, London, 1989.

MONTAGU, A., *The Natural Superiority of Women*. Allen & Unwin, London, 1954.

MORRIS, D., *The Naked Ape: A Zoologist's Study of the Human Animal*. Jonathan Cape, London, 1967.

MORRIS, D., *The Human Zoo*. Jonathan Cape, London, 1969.

MORRIS, D., *Intimate Behaviour*. Jonathan Cape, London, 1971.

MORRIS, D., *Manwatching: a Field Guide to Human Behaviour*. Jonathan Cape, London, 1977.

MORRIS, D., *The Book of Ages*. Jonathan Cape, London, 1983.

MORRIS, D., *Bodywatching: a Field Guide to the Human Species*. Jonathan Cape, London, 1987.

MORRIS, D., *Babywatching*. Jonathan Cape, London, 1991.

MORRIS, D., *Bodytalk: a World Guide to Gestures*. Jonathan Cape, London, 1994.

MORRIS, D., *The Human Animal: a Personal View of the Human Species*. BBC Books, London, 1994.

NICHOLSON, J., *Men and Women. How Different are They?* Oxford University Press, Oxford, 1993.

OAKLEY, A., *Sex, Gender and Society*. Arena, Aldershot, 1972.

ONEN, U., *Ephesus: Ruins and Museum*. Akademia, Izmir, 1983.

PARRY, A., *Tattoo: Secrets of a Strange Art*. Collier Books, New York, 1971.

PENZER, N.M., *The Harem*. Spring Books, London, 1965.

PERADOTTO, J. & SULLIVAN, J.P., *Women in the Ancient World*. State University of the New York Press, Albany, 1984.

PHADNIS, U. & MALANI, I., *Women of the World*. Vikas, New Delhi, 1978.

PINNEY, R., *Vanishing Tribes*. Barker, London, 1968.

PLOSS, H.H., BARTELS, M. & BARTELS, P., *Woman: An Historical, Gynaecological and Anthropological Compendium* (three volumes). Heinemann, London, 1935.

POLHEMUS, T. & PROCTOR, L., *Fashion and Anti-fashion: an Anthropology of Clothing and Adornment*. Thames & Hudson, London, 1978.

POOL, R., *The New Sexual Revolution*. Hodder & Stoughton, London, 1993.

POOL, R., *Eve's Rib*. Crown, New York, 1994.

RAWSON, P., *Primitive Erotic Art*. Putnam, New York, 1973.

RICHARDS, D., *The Penis*. BabyShoe Publications, Kent, 1992.

RIDLEY, M., *The Red Queen. Sex and the Evolution of Human Nature*. Viking, New York, 1993.

ROHRBAUGH, J.B., *Women: Psychology's Puzzle*. Abacus, London, 1981.

ROTHBLATT, M., *The Apartheid of Sex*. Crown, New York, 1995.

SCHEINFELD, A., *Women and Men*. Chatto & Windus, London, 1947.

SCOTT, G.R., *Curious Customs of Sex and Marriage*. Torchstream Books, London, 1953; republished 1995.

SCOTT, G.R., *Phallic Worship*. Luxor Press, London, 1966.

SHORTER, E., *A History of Women's Bodies*. Allen Lane, London, 1983.

SEIBERT, I., *Woman in Ancient Near East*. Edition, Leipzig, 1974.

SMALL, M.F., *What's Love Got To Do With It?* Anchor, New York, 1995.

SMITH, J., *Misogynies*. Faber & Faber, London, 1989.

STANSILL, P. & MAIROWITZ, D.Z., *BAMN (By Any Means Necessary): Outlaw Manifestos and Ephemera 1965-70*. Penguin Books, Middlesex, 1971.

STOLLER, R.J., *Sex and Gender*. Hogarth Press, London, 1968.

SWERDLOFF, P., *Men and Women*. Time-Life, New York, 1976.

Bibliography

SWIGART, J., *The Myth of the Bad Mother*. Doubleday, New York, 1991.

SYNNOTT, A., *The Body Social*. Routledge, London, 1993.

TAVRIS, C. & OFFIR, C., *The Longest War*. Harcourt Brace Jovanovich, New York, 1977.

TIGER, L., *Men in Groups*. Nelson, London, 1969.

TURNBULL, C., *The Forest People*. Jonathan Cape, London, 1961.

TURNER, E. S., *A History of Courting*. Michael Joseph, London, 1954.

TYLDESLEY, J., *Hatchepsut: the Female Pharaoh*. Viking, London, 1995.

VANGGAARD, T., *Phallós: A Symbol and its History in the Male World*. Jonathan Cape, London, 1972.

VERMASEREN, M.J., *Cybele and Attis: the Myth and the Cult*. Thames & Hudson, London, 1977.

WARNER, M., *Alone of All Her Sex: the Myth and the Cult of the Virgin Mary*. Weidenfeld & Nicolson, London, 1976.

WEITZ, S., *Sex Roles*. Oxford University Press, Oxford, 1977.

WESTERMARCK, E., *The History of Human Marriage*. Macmillan, London, 1894.

WILLIAMS, N., *Powder and Paint*. Longmans, London, 1957.

WOLF, N., *The Beauty Myth*. Vintage, London, 1991.

WRAGE, K.H., *Man and Woman*. Collins, London, 1966.

ZACKS, R., *History Laid Bare*. HarperCollins, New York, 1994.

Acknowledgements

This book has been written to accompany the six-part television series made by Partridge Films in association with The Learning Channel in the United States. I owe a debt of gratitude to all the members of the large team that made the programmes. They were, without exception, a joy to work with. Their enthusiasm for the project was unflagging and the immense care and effort they took to record the various patterns of human behaviour all over the globe was inspiring. I offer my special thanks to every one of the people listed below.

For the picture research on this book I am especially grateful for the expert endeavours of Liz Boggis and David Cottingham and, for their editorial expertise, Sheila Ableman and Sally Potter of BBC Books.

Finally, an additional word of thanks to all those who assisted the television production team with expert advice on special subjects.

Television Production Team:

Executive Producers
Sandra Gregory (for The
Learning Channel)
Michael Rosenberg
(for Partridge Films)

Series Producer
Clive Bromhall

Production Manager
Carrie Tooth

Producers
Bonni Cohen (USA)
Clare Hargreaves
John Longley
Beverley Parr

Assistant Producers
Angeline Barraclough-Tan (Asia)
Patricia Sarmiento (Latin America)
Jano Williams (Japan)

Production Co-ordinators
Carmen Cobos
Sarah Feltes (USA)
Ann Holland

Series Researchers
David Mansfield
Kirsten MacLeod
Nicole Newnham (USA)
Stephen Oliver
Alina Paul
Dinah Rogers
MCM Research

Graphic Designer
Matt Carter (4:2:2 Graphics)

Music
Martin Kiszko

Video Editors
Maggie Choyce
Paul Jackson
John Lee
Jake Martin

Sound Recordists
Sara Chin (USA)
Doug Dunderdale (USA)
Alex Marsden
Nick Ware
Alastair Widgery
Simon Wilson

Camera Operators
Sean Bobbitt
Philip Bonham-Carter
Michael Chin
Bob Elfstrom (USA)
Jon Else (USA)
Simon Everson
Terry Hopkins (USA)
Ferne Pearlstein (USA)
Alphonse Roy
Jon Shenk (USA)

Consultants
Erika Rauschenbach
Misha Bykoff
Sanjeev Misra
Anuradha Awasthi
Soco Aquilar

249

Picture Credits

BBC Books would like to thank the following for providing photographs and for permission to reproduce copyright material. While every effort has been made to trace and acknowledge all copyright holders, we would like to apologize should there have been any errors or omissions.

Key: T – top, C – centre, B – bottom, L – left, R – right, TL – top left, TR – top right, BL – bottom left, BR – bottom right

ALLSPORT page 230 (T, Al Bello, and B, Tony Duffy); ANCIENT ART AND ARCHITECTURE COLLECTION pages 30/31 and 94/95; BRITSTOCK page 19 (TL, TR and C); CLIVE BROMHALL pages 7, 11, 15, 19 (B), 27 (B), 71 (R), 74, 90, 102, 107, 114/115, 159, 178, 186, 199, 202, 222/3, and 235 (B); CADBURY'S CRUNCHIE FLYING CIRCUS WINGWALKING TEAM page 231; FRITZI DROSTEN page 187; FORMAT page 154 (Judy Harrison); ROBERT HARDING pages 47 (Yan Layma), 106/107 (Adam Woolfitt), 171 (Ian Griffiths) and 198 (Victor Engelbert); CLARE HARGREAVES pages 130/131 and 139; HULTON GETTY page 218; HUTCHISON LIBRARY pages 42 (T, Leslie Woodhead), 43 (R, Jeremy Horner), 146 (Harriet Logan), 147 (B, Liba Taylor) and 190 (Sarah Errington); ROB HYAMS DESIGN page 79; IMAGE BANK pages 51 (Infocus) and 243 (Alex Stewart); KATZ pages 83 (Marco Pesaresi/Contrasto), 98/99 (Marco Pesaresi/Contrasto) and 118/119 (Michael Schumann/Saba); MAGNUM pages 66/67 (Ernst Haas), 166 (Raghu Rai), 203 (Abbas) and 206/207 (Abbas); DESMOND MORRIS page 147 (T); NET-WORK pages 74/75 (Wojtek Buss/Rapho), 138 (Steber/JB Pictures) and 235 (T, Hans Silvester/Rapho); ONLY HORSES page 22; 'PA' NEWS page 219; PANOS PICTURES page 174 (Ron Giling); REX FEATURES pages 14 (Peter Stumpf), 22/23, 27 (T, Rick Falco), 42 (B), 43 (L, Vic Thomasson), 46 (Aral), 54 (BL and BR, Catherine de Wolfe), 55 (Gerald Davis), 71 (L, P.P. Harnett), 99 (T, Jeffrey R. Werner; B), 127 (B, Peter Brooker), 155, 183, 207, 215 (B, Lehtikuva Oy), and 239 (David White); SKYSCAN BALLOON PHOTOGRAPHY page 62; FRANK SPOONER PICTURES pages 58 (Ducey), 123 (Alexis Duclos), 135 (Esaias Baitel), 143 (Ferry/Liaison), 163 (Robert Ricci) and 223 (Everke/Liaison); STILL PICTURES pages 127 (T, Genevieve Renson) and 174/175 (Mark Edwards); TONY STONE IMAGES pages 18 (Bruce Herman), 182/183 (Penny Tweedie), 190/191 (Walter Hodges), 215 (T, Peter Correz) and 238 (Howard Grey); TRIUMPH INTERNATIONAL page 54 (T).

Index

Page numbers in *italic* refer to
the illustrations

abortion 189, 227
Afghanistan 172, 205
Ainu 70
Al Azhar, Sheikh of 210
Amsterdam 82, *83*
Aquinas, Thomas 148
Assam 70
Assyrians 205
availability 73–7, 110

baby-bonder 177–8, *178*
Baka 84, 196
Bali *147*, 149, 228
baptism 132
basil 76
battered wives 194–5
beard 26, 53
beauty 40–51
bee-sting lips *42*, 43
belly-dancing *46*
bicycle *34*, 35
birth 25, 169–70
Bobbit case 225–6
body-building, female *230*
body-piercing *71*, 72–3
boxing, female 229–32, *230*
Brazil 226
breasts 26–8, *27*, 41, 44–5, 52,
 58, 80, 197
brothels 82, 97–101, *102*

bulitas 60
Bulwer, John 71–2
bum-bra 52, *54*
Burma 44, 71, 72
Burton, Sir Richard 208
buttocks 52

California 216, 234
Calment, Madame Jeanne
 162–3, *163*
Cameroon 44, 104
cantalores 234
Catholic Church 116, 117
celibacy 116–17, 120, 189, 224
Cerne Abbas Giant *62–3*, 65
Cerridwen Fallingstar 216
chastity 138
chastity belt 78–80, *79*
cheerleaders 59
Chesterfield, Lord 237
Chicago 220
chimpanzee 24–5, 26
China 45, 172–3
Christian Church 71, 100, 236,
 240
Cinderella 45
circumcision (female) 81,
 132–6, *207*, 209–10
circumcision (male) 68, 134–6,
 135
Cledalism 123–4
Colombia *146–7*, 158, 234
colour-blindness 16

Constantine, Captain 72
contraception 189, 227
Corsica 64
cosmetics 57–9
cosmetic surgery *see* face-lifts
courage 70–3
Covenant of the Goddess 216
co-wives 108, 111–12, 179–80
crèches 178–9
Crusades 78, 116–17

Dad-to-Dad 177
Dali, Salvador 123–4
dancing 59–60
death 165–7
Dekker, Thomas 237
Deng Xiaoping 173
depression 16
Diana of Ephesus 200–1, *202*
Dianic Cult 240
divorce 90–1, *90*
djambia 140
domestic violence 194–5
Down's Syndrome 192–3
dowry 156, 157–8, 172
dying rooms 173
dyslexia 36

E-Fit 16
Egypt 43, 57, 64, 68, 88,
 134, 210
Egyptian Organization of
 Human Rights 210

Enki 200
Ephesus 97, *102*
Estonia 88–9, 128, 158
Ethiopia 41, 140
evil eye 152, 153, 156
eyefolds 69
eyes 57

face 15–16, 48–50
face-bleaching 68
face-lifts 53–6, *54*
facial hair *22–3*, 25–6, 53
Fagundes, Geraldo 226
faldetta 74, 76
fat 16–17
fatwa 210
feast 126–8, *127*
feet 41, 45–8, 155
female rebellion 216–20
feminist movement 217, *219*
feminists 48, 236
fertility, 192, *199*
Filipinos 60, 172
fine-tuning 181–8
Finland 214, *215*
fire-fighting, female 234
Florence 78
flower language *74–5*, 77, 153,
  156
foetus 36, 168
Fon of Mankon 104
food-gathering *11*, 32
foot-binding 45, *47*
France 185
fruit-carrying 13–15, *15*

gay weddings *118–19*, 120
geishas 17
gender bias 12, 172–6, 189,
  232

gender separation 136–7
gender signals 20, 25–6, 49
genitals 20–5, 60, 61, 81,
  134–6, 197, 209–10
genius 38
giraffe-necks *43*, 44
go-karting 33
Golden Lotus 45
Goodhart, Charles 38
gorilla 24–5
grandparents 164, 180
Greece 17, 53, 64, 97, 128–9,
  132, 149, 156, 211
Guillotine Movement 226
Guinness Book of Records 26
gypsies 149

hair-straightening 68–9
Hammersmith Hospital 181
harems 103–5, 109
health 16, 49, 57–60
hearing 17, 185
henna 155–6, *155*
Highland Games 13, *14*
Hindus 149, 165, 232
hips 25, 44, 56–7, 197
homosexuals 117, 120–2
honeymoon 214, *215*
Horace 97
horses 35
house-husbands 176–7
Housewife Solution 188–9, 192
Houston 138
hunting *11*, 32, *30–1*
Hyattsville, Maryland 149

Il-Quccija 133–4
India 64, 68, 93, *94–5*, 112,
  149, 150, 157, 165–7, 172,
  232

Institute of Islamic
  Information 111
intelligence 29, 37–9, 241
internet 86, 124
Irabo 80
Islam 111–12, 208, 210
Istanbul 103

Jaipur *106*
Japan 29, 64–5, *66–7*, 69,
  96, *99*, 211, 228–9
jealousy 77, 103, 108, 109, 110,
  116, 180
Jefferson, Thomas 121
Jerome, St 148
Johns Hopkins University,
  Baltimore 36
Joseph, Alex 108

Kabul 205
Kaiser Hospital 185–8
Kalyan Ramji Sain 25–6
Kama Sutra 93
kangaroo care 185–8, *187*
karate 233
khat 160
Knight, Chris 151
knights 64, 116–17
Komaka-shi 64
Koran 111, 132, 149, 205, 210
Kresty Prison 125
Kuan Ying 234

Langseth, Hans 26
Lanzarote 77
lap-dancing *27*
larynx 28
Las Vegas 101
Late Breeding Solution 192–3
leg-crossing 19–20, *19*

lesbians 112, 189, 224
life span 53, 126, 161–5, 180, 192
lingam 64
lip-plates 41–3, *42*
lips 41, *42*, 43
Little Mother 180–1, *182–3*
Los Angeles 100
Love Hotels 96–7, *99*

Macho Society of Brazil 226
Madras 232
Malta 64, *74*, 76, 133, *159*, 197, *199*
Maori 71
Marquesans 71, 112–16
masturbation 224
Maternal Solution 176–81, 188–93
Mattos case 226
menopause 180, 192
menstruation 144, 145–52, *147*, 228, 237
mental differences 29–39
Milan University 179
Mohammed 205–8
Mongo Faya 104–5, *107*
monks 116, 117, 120, 121, 164, 237
monogamy 88, 108, 110, 111, 165, 180
Mormons 105–8, 179
Moscow 86, 100
Mother Goddess 64, 196–203, *199*, 234–40
moustache 22–3, 25–6
Mursi 41, 140–1
muscle 12–15
Museum of Menstruation 149–50
Muslims 108–9, 149, 167, 205, 210–11, 233

Naga 70
National Organization for Women 217
neck 41, 43–4, *43 see also* giraffe-necks
Nevada 100–1
Nigeria 80
Non-Breeding Solution 120, 121, 189, 192
non-reproductive sex 116–22
Novello da Carrara 78
nuns 117, 120, 121, 164, 208, 232–3, 237

Old Religion 236–7, 240
oral contraceptive 226

Padaung 44
paedophilia 117
pagan weddings 216–17
pair-bond 24, 82, 85, 87–91, 97, 101, 103, 109, 110, 113, 117, 120, 124–5, 152, 160, 194, 196
pair-formation 152–8
Pakistan 132–3, 172
Palace of the Winds, Jaipur *106*
Paris 78, 100
pelvic girdle 17–20
penis 21, 24, 60–5, *62–3*
penis enlargement 61
phallus 60–5, *66–7*, 200, 220–1, *223*, 225
Philippines 60, 172
Pinçus, Gregory 226
Plastercasters 220–1, *223*, 225
play-fighting *51*
Plutarch 17
PMS (premenstrual syndrome)

151–2
polyandry 103, 111, 112–16, *114–15*
polygamy 103–112
polygyny 103, 104, 105–8, 106–7, 109–12, 179–80
pornography 124
priests, female *238–9*
prostitution 82–4, 97–101, *98–9 see also* window-girls
puberty 137–45, 146–7
pygmies 10–12, *11*, 84, 196

qat 160
Quickcourt 90–1, *90*
Quinceanera 137–8, *138*

riding 20
risk-taking 13, 32, 33, 73, 233
rock-climbing 242, *243*
Rome 53, 64
running 17–19, *18*
Russia 86

St Anne's Convent, Madras 232–3
St Petersburg 125
Samoa 71, *78*
San Francisco *118–19*, 120, 122, 185, 236
Saudi Arabia 204–5, 208
scarification 141
SCUM (Society for Cutting Up Men) 217–20
secondary mateship 113–16
sex ratio 172–3, *217*
sex toys 96, 122–3
sexual equality 214, *238*, 241
sexual givers 221
sexual takers 221–4

shaving 53
shoes 45–8
side-saddle 20, *22*
Singapore 69, 167, 234
sitting 19–20
smell 17, 184–5
Smithsonian Institute, Washington 26
sodomy 121
Solanas, Valerie 220
solitary sex 122–4, *123*, 189
Spain 149
Spatial Solution 188, *190–1*, 192
sperm 24, 193
sperm-count 193
spiders 33–5
status display 65–9
sterilization 189
striptease, male *222–3*
stuttering 35–6
suffrage movement 217, *218*
Suggs, Robert 116
suicide 16
Sumer 200
Sundargarth, 26
Surma 41
suttee 165–7, *166*
Sweden 37
symmetry 49–50

Tahiti *74–5*, 109

Taliban movement 205
Tartars 72
Tarxien 197, *199*
tattoos 70–2, *71*, 141, 145
Tempest, Helen 234
Temporal Solution 192
Tennyson, Alfred, Lord 237
testicles 21–5
Texas 229
Thailand 44, 211
Tiny Tots Beauty Pageant *55*, 56
Toda 112–16, *114–15*
tooth-filing 141
Topkapi Palace 103
touch 17
Tuareg 68
Turkey 97, 103–4, 134–5, *135*, 200

uncircumcising 136
urban mothers 171–2, *171, 174–5*
Utah 105

Van Gogh, Vincent 162
Varanasi 167
veil 132, 140, 152, *203*, 204–9, *206–7*, 211 *see also faldetta*
verbal abilities 17, 35–6, 37
virginity 77–81, 133, 137, 142, 152, 157, 213, 214

Virgin Mary 201, 234, *235*
visual abilities 12, 35, 36–7
voice 28–9
voodoo *235*

waist 56–7
wandering eye 91–7
walking 17
Warhol, Andy 220
Wayuu 144–5, *146–7*, 158
weddings 120, 128, 152–60, *154*, 212–14
Wicca 236, 240
wife-battering 194–5
wife-carrying contest 214, *215*
Wilde, Oscar 121
window-girls 82, *83*
wine-tasting 185, *186*
wing-walking, female *231*, 233–4
witches 65, 167, 216, 236–40
Wolf, Naomi 48–9
wrestling 228–9

Yakusa 71
Yemen *130–1*, 132, *139*, 140, 158, 160–1, 204
York Mystery Plays 234–6
Yosemite National Park 242, *243*
youth 49, 51–7